CRITICAL FOUNDATIONS

Copyright © 2022 Scott Schimmel

All rights reserved. Just don't mess with the content, okay?

ISBN-9798412256498

Printed in the United States of America

www.theyouschool.com
Edited by: Beth Schimmel
Cover Design by: The Author

CRITICAL FOUNDATIONS

*THE 30 QUESTIONS EVERYONE MUST
ANSWER TO BUILD A MEANINGFUL LIFE*

SCOTT SCHIMMEL

*To my kids, Cale, Grace, and Jane- I hope the life your mom and I have been living is enough to give you the foundation to build your own meaningful lives.
May you never wonder who I really am, or question if I love who you are.*

CONTENTS

Introduction

Part One: The Critical Questions
   Section One: The Critical Identity Questions
   Section Two: The Critical Purpose Questions
   Section Three: The Critical Belonging Questions

Part Two: Rethinking What Kids Need

Conclusion

Acknowledgments

About the Author

INTRODUCTION

Nobody Worries About the Kid Who Wants to Be an Accountant When They Grow Up

Early in high school, I made the declaration to my parents that I was going to pursue a career in Accounting or Finance. One key influence was seeing my older sister stressed out to get perfect grades to go to med school someday. I thought to myself: "there has to be a better way to navigate to the future without trying so hard." Also, through experiencing the financial success of my parents and relatives in South Orange County and the comfort and respect it brought- I felt the pressure to be successful in the same way. Plus, after watching a Michael J. Fox character on the 80's family sitcom *Family Ties* get all the laughs because he was remarkably mature, conservative, and focused on business success (he read the Wall Street Journal, so I started to read it, too)- I knew Accounting or Finance was the safest choice for my future. It made too much sense! When you're a teenager growing up in my family, in my town, and you say out loud:

"Gee whiz, when I grow up, I want to go into finance!" not only does nobody second guess you, but you get a ton of praise and admiration.

The grand plan I hatched for my life, which I spent the next seven years relentlessly focused on, came on a whim to relieve myself of stress and anxiety- and nobody challenged it. I look back now and wish someone had. Those seven years weren't a waste- I earned a valuable college degree, I had six internships in accounting and finance, and I discovered later on through mentoring, self-reflection, and risky trial-and-error that a meaningful life for me was down a different path. The biggest regret I have is that I pursued success through the perspective of others rather than listen to my own inner voice.

Looking back, I have no regrets. But, the biggest critique I have is that I didn't have the tools to construct that framework for myself until much later.

Here's a sad reality: you can do well in school, get into a great school, do well there, get a well-paying job, but **still miss out on building a meaningful life**. It happens all the time. I bet you can think of a lot of people who fit that bill.

The school system is not set up for students to build a meaningful life. It's a sprint to gain the knowledge necessary to pass tests and be ready for the academic challenges in college. There's little room for reflection, integration, or deliberate self-awareness building. **You can be successful in school but not know yourself or have a clear picture of what a meaningful life could look like for yourself.** You can get accepted into the top universities but miss out on the essential parts of growing up well.

Taking a step back, two fundamental beliefs that drive me:

1. *Every kid has the inherent potential to be successful.*
2. *Every kid deserves the opportunity to construct a meaningful life for themselves.*

Neither of those will come to fruition without intentional design and conscious commitment. Every kid requires intervention and guidance- no student is successful on their own, no student will construct a meaningful life unless guided. That's where school, family, and the broader community come in. We have an opportunity and the responsibility to guide students to success and meaning for their lives. (And, yes, those two should always overlap.)

Self-reflection is the critical skill students need to construct a meaningful life for themselves. Unless and until we provide frequent opportunities to reflect on what they're learning about themselves and the world, they will be mindlessly going down a path of least resistance, whatever that may be for that student.

But what is a meaningful life?

Through years of research and work with tens of thousands of students, educators, and parents, we've developed a keen perspective- building a meaningful life *is the point*, but it's not what the system is currently designed for. It has to be intentionally constructed.

What is the goal? It starts with getting clear about what it looks like in regular, relatable terms. There are three pillars to the foundation of a meaningful life:

1. A clear **identity**
2. A compelling **purpose**

3. Authentic **connection**

Constructing a clear identity is the primary pursuit of adolescence. Most of the journey, though, is off track. Teenagers look to their peers and mainstream media to give them answers to who they are, what's most important, and what the world is all about. A clear identity consists of your fundamental beliefs, core values, and a clear picture of who you are and who you're not. It can't come from the outside, although finding real-life illustrations will help. You have to search inward and do the honest work of looking in the mirror and accepting what you see.

Finding a compelling purpose is also something that can't come from external sources. As the saying goes, if you don't find your purpose, you'll play a part in someone else's. A compelling purpose is the mixture of your unique talents, strengths, interests, energy, wiring, and irritation. What you have to offer in terms of your assets and capabilities, combined with a deep desire to solve a problem, will bring you to the epicenter of an inner drive that makes you come alive and fix your focus.

Building authentic relationships, of course, is central to a meaningful life. Can you imagine someone who's confident about their identity and purpose but does not have anyone to share life with? Can you picture someone who's deeply satisfied with their work yet lives each day without anyone to lean on?

The question then becomes: *how do you help young people discover their identity, find their purpose, and have the ingredients to build authentic relationships?* **Can you teach someone these pillars like we would teach social studies or a language?**

Unfortunately, these three pillars require a custom design for each person, making it much more challenging to scale a learning paradigm.

Who's to say what should be most important to someone? How do you tell people who they are and what's worth their life's investment? Even coming from a particularly formed philosophy or religious perspective, there are dynamics of passing those tenets and principles that must be discovered rather than told.

Through two decades of work with teenagers, college students, transitioning veterans, and corporate executives, we've learned that the only way that works to guide someone to clarity is to create the circumstances for them to discover their own answers to life's most important questions. It doesn't work to give answers- we have to ask the questions. And expect them to discover answers.

We've identified a series of questions for each pillar that will yield clarity, confidence, and the foundation for building a meaningful life if answered through a simple process over time. Here's our core premise: if kids can articulate their answers to these series of questions, we believe they will have a strong foundation for constructing a life that's both poised for success and prepared for meaning.

ANSWERS TO LIFE'S MOST IMPORTANT QUESTIONS

We want the absolute best for our kids, don't we? Not only do we want them to build a life on their own someday and get off the payroll, but we also want them to be happy, to be safe, to be well-adjusted and good, kind people.

But how confident are you that your kids have what they need to make that a reality?

I remember the first time I felt like a real adult— it was when my wife (then girlfriend) and I went to a jewelry store to look into buying an engagement ring. We were only 22 years old, and I was convinced that someone from the back of the store would confront us and ask why we thought we belonged there. We still felt like kids, but something shifted when we left the store with a diamond.

There were other significant moments, too: the first time I rented a car on my own, the first time I signed home loan documents, and the first time my wife had an ultrasound. Every moment was a weird feeling- I knew I was doing adult-like things, but inside I still felt like I was playing pretend.

That begs the question: when are you considered an adult?
- *Is it when you reach a certain age?*
- *Is it when you've graduated from high school? Or is it college?*
- *Are you an adult when you can pay your bills?*

The judicial system says you're an adult at 18, the car companies say you're an adult at 25, and the airlines say you're an adult at 2 (they make you pay for your own seat, at least).

But just because your age has crossed a threshold, does that mean you're a proper adult?

Once, while coaching a Little League baseball game for my eight-year-old son, an opposing coach (who looked like he was at least fifty) invited me to "meet me in the parking lot" after the game because he thought I unfairly influenced the fourteen-year-old umpire during a close play at the plate.

Another time I got an angry email from a parent whose kid went through a YouSchool session because I had emailed her a video her daughter made but didn't get permission from her daughter first. In all fairness, I had lost her daughter's email address but had explicitly told the students I would send them the videos we made where they shared their 'life story' over a three-minute video. The girl was frustrated that I sent it directly to her parents because she wanted to be the one to send it. Her mom's email to me had 17 paragraphs (I counted) filled with accusations, swear words, and threats of my reputation ruined if I ever "lied to another child" again.

You can be an adult according to your age or stage in life, but you can be far from healthy or well-adjusted. You can make plenty of money and own your own home and have your own kids, but still be far off from the kind of maturity or heart that most of us would agree defines a healthy, good person. I'm sure you have stories about people you know, too.

We've been paying a lot of attention over the past few years to learning about the process and developmental thresholds that define adulthood. We've worked up close with thousands of students in high school making life decisions about what to do after they graduate. We've journeyed alongside thousands of college students taking steps towards a career. We've coached hundreds of transitioning military to redesign their lives post-service. Ultimately, all those life stages are about growing up, something few people learn how to do specifically. Most people just go through the motions, try to live up to the expectations people have of someone at their age, and hope it all works out later.

We've been in the trenches with thousands of young people- hearing what's on their minds, learning from their experiences, and watching the decisions they make.

We've been doing a lot of research, too, from some of the sharpest minds regarding human development:

- Dan McAdams and Narrative Identity Formation

- Viktor Frankl's logotherapy (The concentration camp survivor and psychotherapist who wrote *Man's Search for Meaning*)
- Trauma-Informed Care / Practices from Peter Levine
- The Search Institute's Developmental Assets Framework
- Dan Goleman's Emotional Intelligence work
- CASEL's five social-emotional competencies
- Dan Siegel's adolescent brain development and attachment theory

Combined with research and years of boots-on-the-ground experience, we've developed a unique, common-sense point of view. **What we need to do is redefine the point of growing up.**

Redefining adulthood means we have a different set of parameters to define success. We're using an outdated model. Right now, we define adulthood as an age or a stage. We evaluate preparedness based on academic outcomes and diplomas. We look at a person who's employed and make false assumptions. Just because you can conjugate some verbs, do high-level calculus, enlist in the military, or get to work on time doesn't mean you're living life to the fullest.

Everyone needs guiding, prompted questions, expecting to respond with a clear, convincing answer. It's not content or solutions they need- it's questions.

Students need to be challenged to answer life's most important questions. The best environment for them to answer them is simple: first, show them. Students need to have the adults invested in their lives demonstrate what authentic answers sound like. Teachers, parents, principals, and coaches go first. Next, they need some time and quiet space to think for themselves. After that, they need to share with their peers-both in disclosing their thoughts and hearing from their peers, they will be able to both clarify and navigate to answers that most deeply resonate with themselves.

The process is simple. It's repeatable. Every parent, every teacher, every coach, and youth worker can learn how to lead it. The best way to show it is to engage in the work yourself.

You can already be an adult according to your age or stage in life, and it's the perfect time to figure it all out- yourself, the world, and your place in it. It's never too late. Right now could be your moment to answer life's most pressing questions, to do the difficult work of self-reflection and discovery to come up with your answers. I hope you receive this book as your invitation and roadmap to do just that.

Even more so, I hope that you not only engage in the guided prompts within these pages and do what kids need the most- adults in their lives who are modeling and demonstrating an authentic life and choosing to invest in theirs. But that you choose to move towards kids through personal relationships and ask them these questions. It might be awkward, but it will be worth it.

EXISTENTIAL VACUUM

Do you ever get 'The Sunday Blues'? It's that icky feeling we all sometimes get when we're feeling bored, unsettled, and stuck. Growing up, my sister and I called it 'that homesick feeling' we would sometimes get like we knew we weren't in a place where we belonged. Everyone gets the feeling. You get it, I get it, and our kids get it.

Students will fill the void they feel, but will they fill it well?

Viktor Frankl was an Austrian Neurologist and Psychiatrist (Medical Doctor and Psychiatrist) who was sent to Auschwitz and three other concentration camps during World War II because he was Jewish. He experienced terrible loss with the death of his parents and his wife. But, he survived and came out of the camps to write *A Man's Search For Meaning*, a global bestselling book describing his experiences of the atrocities. The book is filled with insights about why some people clung to hope and survived while others died.

Frankl developed a framework to support people through suffering and to help explain how all of life works. He says we all have a "will to meaning" in our lives- an innate drive to find a purpose and a reason for being. One of the key ways he proposed to help us build a meaningful life is to engage with our own 'existential vacuum.'

An existential vacuum is the feeling we all get of hopelessness, meaninglessness, a stuck-in-the-moment with no foresight for relief. It's a disconnection from creativity, from bonding to others, from opportunities to use your talents for the sake of someone else.

Maybe you feel the existential vacuum on a Sunday afternoon when you think about going to work the next day. Perhaps it's on your commute home after spending all day in meetings that felt inefficient and repetitive. Or maybe it's in those rare moments of reflection when you hear about someone's death, and you wonder what kind of legacy you'll leave.

The existential vacuum is a feeling.
We all get it.
It's common to the human experience.

What does it feel like to you? Some say boredom. Others say loneliness. Or anxiety. Thoughts creep in: you don't have what it takes // you're all alone // no one cares about you // nothing you do matters // this is too hard // this isn't the way it's supposed to be...

Where do you go when you feel it- what does it drive you to do? Entertainment? Social media? Work? Cleaning? Shaming yourself. Criticizing others? A review of your bank account or how many followers you have? Envy of others?

The temptation will always be to fill that void you feel with something that falls short of what you indeed desire. You'll be tempted to pursue:

- *Career Success.*
- *Respect from others.*
- *Products from Magnolia.*
- *Security.*
- *People thinking well and highly of you.*
- *Being busy.*
- *A higher degree.*
- *Cryptocurrency.*
- *Abs.*
- *Subway tile in your bathroom.*
- *The latest yoga pants.*
- *Running a sprint triathlon.*
- *A Tesla.*
- *A trip to Tulum.*
- *A scratch handicap.*

None of those accomplishments, products, experiences, or possessions will fill your life with meaning. They're distractions. And yet, most of what we pursue, search for on the internet, scroll through on Instagram, and invest in focuses on those trivial things. We model those pursuits to the next generation, too.

Adults feel the existential vacuum, and so do teenagers. Really, that's when the deeper questioning starts for most. Teens today are particularly prone to wondering what the point of life is all about.

They've been exposed to extraordinary events like financial crashes, political upheaval, a global pandemic, worsening racial tension, natural disasters, and rampant selfishness and immaturity from leaders. Sure, previous generations saw horrible global scenarios, too. But there's an edge out there that borders on collective nihilism. At least that's where the culture seems to be headed.

That is unless we can figure out a way to guide the next generation into deeper reflection and a wise framework for them to build their lives on faith, hope, and love.

As bold and audacious as it sounds, that's what we're trying to do through the YouSchool- give young people and the adults who care about them a roadmap for building a life that's deeply meaningful and practically relevant to bring good to the world.

In the meantime, I invite you to pay attention to your own existential vacuum. Here's what you can do to use that icky, empty feeling for your good:

- Understand it as an indicator. A prompt. A trigger. That feeling is trying to tell you something. It's trying to get your attention.
- Embrace it. Explore it. Befriend it. Be curious about it. Have a conversation with it.
- Make observations about it. Depersonalize the feeling as just something that comes and goes, like hunger or thirst.

- Talk with other people about it. Share the feeling you get with your friends. Talk about it with your kids.

The existential vacuum is an invitation, really. It's an invitation to take inventory of your life and the arc of your story. It's a reminder that there's something more, something more profound- and only that will truly satisfy your soul. Feeling lonely, empty, bored, or lost are the symptoms of a problem and indicate a more fitting, centered, and whole way to live.

THE OPTIONS FOR LIFE

Parents tell their children to pursue happiness. Later on, we'll explore together why telling your kids you want them to be happy can be so damaging and unhelpful. But, for now, let's explore the different options that are available for teens as they move forward in life because there are other, competing paths they need to choose, whether they're aware of them or not:

1. **The Survival Life:** some families have dealt with extraordinary circumstances- financial challenges, trouble with the law, health, traumatic and dangerous living environments, abuse, etc, that the imagination they share with the next generation is a life of survival. The primary emphasis is on taking care of yourself, getting a job to earn some money, staying safe, and getting out of harm's way.
2. **The Responsible Life:** many families communicate to their kids that the primary aim and most important expectation is for the next generation to act responsibly. That might look like taking over the family business, taking care of each other, taking care of the older generation, or fulfilling career expectations. If you want to do well in life, you need to do what's expected of you, pay

your bills, clean up your yard, and pay your taxes. Work is seen as an opportunity to fulfill expectations other people have of your potential.

3. **The Comfortable Life:** some families, especially those who generationally are moving their way up the economic ladder, stress the importance of creating a comfortable life and avoiding stress or headaches. Work is a means to purchasing power to prevent discomfort.

4. **The Happy Life:** this is confusing because it's so vague, but most families are hoping to prepare their kids for a happy life. Rarely defined, it usually lands in the ballpark of financial success, avoidance of conflict or strife, and the ability to take luxurious vacations and live in gated neighborhoods. Work is a means to provide for perks.

5. **The Fulfilling Life**: for parents who made mistakes in their life path, whether in career or marriage or otherwise, they often share a message with their kids to pursue fulfillment. Don't go after money or responsibility, they say. Make a run after a career and a lifestyle that makes you come alive and fulfills your passion. Work is a means to express yourself, your values, and your desires.

6. **The Meaningful Life**: the rarest of them all, this is the path that invites kids to participate in a cause or a mission bigger than themselves. It's an invitation to fight for something, to solve a problem, to contribute to the greater good, and to leave a legacy. It's a life that talks little about comfort or happiness or fulfillment, although the few that walk this path would say they're delighted and fulfilled- and far from comfortable. These are the kinds of

people who seem to get younger every year, continuously learning and growing and looking forward to ways to contribute each day.

When you look at those options, it's helpful to view them as a mirror to your own experiences and perspectives. What were you taught by the generation who raised you? What have you pursued? Most importantly, what have your kids been exposed to, and how could we shift their perspective if they haven't been shown what we hope for them?

In Part One of this book, we will start walking through the Critical Foundations for constructing a meaningful life. Thirty questions need to be answered by kids as they go through adolescence if you want them to obtain the self-awareness, confidence, and direction they need. These are questions that you ought to ask yourself, too. They remain open throughout life since they're questions rather than answers, ideas, or bullet points. These questions become vital for every new stage or season you enter to make the most informed decisions. Kids will watch you as you struggle to answer them and learn from you as you settle on answers that deeply resonate and provide value to your life.

In Part Two, we'll spend time thinking about this unique generation- their assets and liabilities, as well as what they need from parents and adults involved in their lives. We'll address what effective intervention looks like, in response to our decade working with students inside school systems and after school programs.

My hope is that you consider this book a workbook for you as much as it can be a curriculum guide for your work with students, whether as a parent, educator, or coach. This is the way life works best- together, on the journey, through engagement, humility, and courage.

SCOTT SCHIMMEL

PART ONE: THE CRITICAL QUESTIONS

SECTION ONE:
THE CRITICAL IDENTITY QUESTIONS

The first pillar for constructing a meaningful life is about your **identity**- who you are, what makes you unique, and what matters most to you. Your identity is about your fundamental beliefs, values, and understanding of your place in the world. It determines how you view yourself and how you interact with everyone around you.

Here's the most exciting part to me- there are clear-cut answers to all of these questions, especially if you've ever hung out with a religious or faith community or lean more towards the scientific community. Who am I? Easy- I'll read you a passage. What should I believe? Here, let me show you some data. What makes me unique? Grab a pencil and this personality assessment, and in 40 minutes, I'll tell you exactly.

The problem is, that's not how humans work when it comes to learning. We don't need to be given answers or told who we are, we have to discover it for ourselves.

In the following chapters, we'll address each question on its own- why it's important, what's underneath it, and what could happen if someone comes up with a confident answer. Each of these questions is critical. Every question has an answer. If answered, you will see significant benefits to your life both now and in the future. However, these questions always remain open. Unlike the way a school is designed- where you answer a question and move on, these questions are ones you will return to repeatedly throughout your life.

How do you answer these questions? Simple- you just start responding. It helps to write your thoughts down on paper. It really helps to share your thoughts out loud. And it really, really helps to hear other people answer the questions for themselves. There's a mirroring effect that will happen, where you'll start to see your answers more clearly as you listen to others.

Now, let's get started.

01: Where have you come from and how has it shaped your life?
KNOWING YOUR BACKSTORY

"Tell us about yourself."

Can you think of a more anxiety-provoking question? On the one hand, it's a softball question, right? Who else knows more about your own life than you? But, rarely does anyone answer this question in a clear, concise, or exciting way. Most people drag on for too long, telling way too many insignificant details. Others skip the most important, relevant parts (remember Seinfeld's "yada, yada, yada"?). Rarely, if ever, do we get to hear someone talk about their life story that has an integrated narrative thread- a fancy way of saying it all makes sense. Why is it so rare to hear someone talk about themselves in a practical, memorable way?

I once heard a 20 year veteran Navy SEAL say, "I'd way rather be in combat getting shot at than to have to talk about myself in an interview."

Growing up, we get the message that it's inappropriate to talk about ourselves and grab the limelight. Everyone knows someone who talks about themselves too much. Nobody wants to be 'that guy.' Also, at our core, we all want to avoid humiliation, embarrassment, or shame at all costs. If we provoke attention, people will look at us, and we might be overwhelmed by their rejection.

But mostly, none of us get taught how to talk about ourselves in an effective way that doesn't make us come across as self-indulgent or narcissistic. We don't get the opportunity to reflect on and understand our past, to process through to find or make meaning from our backstory, or the chance to practice telling our own story in a safe environment.

Whether in a job interview, first date, cocktail party or in the stands at a Little League game, we all get asked to talk about who we are. The question comes in different forms, like "Where are you from?" Or, "So, what do you do?" No matter how it's asked, the direction is the same- they want to hear about who you are and where you come from. Of course, you can answer with the town you were born in or the details about how you moved around a lot- but what do those answers really say about you?

People want to know who you are. They want to get a sense of where you come from and how it's shaped your life. They want to understand the key events and moments that have had a lasting impact on who you are, and who you're becoming. They want to hear about obstacles you've overcome, and failures you've pushed through.

For most people, it takes time to figure out how to talk about yourself. There's no formula, and no one else can script the answer for you. You have to do the process first.

Also, you can't start writing a meaningful story with your life until you make sense of where you come from and how it's shaped you. Even the most boring backstory is still complex. If you explore your past and get to know your backstory, a few important things happen:

- **Clarified Direction**: you're able to see where your life is headed and the path you're on- it's called a trajectory. When you're a teen, it's essential to make a series of decisions that will influence the direction your life takes. Most students don't take the time to think about the overarching path they're on already. No one invents their life from thin air- we all come from a people, a place, and a set of circumstances that are already influencing where we're headed. The more we see the thread of meaning in our backstory, the more we'll be able to see how that thread plays out.
- **Social Capital**: you're able to tell your story more compellingly, become more persuasive, & become someone others can trust. Storytellers always win- they are more likable, friendly, and influential. Many people assume that being a compelling storyteller is an innate gift- some have it, and some don't. Instead, good storytellers are made- they think about their life through the lens of stories and practice telling stories a lot. The more they do, the more feedback they get and the more effective they become.
- **Wellbeing through Integration**: you're able to heal from past wounds, so they fuel who you become rather than act as anchors. A core therapy model practiced by thousands of therapists worldwide asks clients to retell their past experiences and reflect on how they might connect. The model invites people to recall memories, significantly divergent memories, and reflect on how they relate to each other. Our brains and bodies store memories inefficiently- all over the place- and in the process of telling our past stories, we can find connections that we hadn't previously made. That moment when you see a pattern or see a link is what most would call an insight or an 'aha moment.' Internally, our brains integrate stored memories, becoming more efficient and effective at seeing patterns. It's the foundation for mental health and wellbeing.

- **Stronger Agency**: knowing your backstory will empower you to pick up the pen to write a life story that's consistent with your true self. You won't feel like life is happening to you like you are at the mercy of events and circumstances thrown your way. You'll see an overarching narrative structure to your life, and you'll even recognize the decisions you made in your past, even unconsciously, determine what happened. The more you reflect on the past choices you made, the more you'll realize at the moment that an inflection point is upon you. You'll feel more confident that you are authoring your life story.

Doing a deep dive into your backstory will help you on many levels. You'll be able to talk about yourself in a clear, compelling way. Other people will know who you are and learn how to interact with you. You will integrate some divergent experiences and ideas from your past. You'll have greater clarity on how to make better choices for your life. You'll feel more confident in your agency.

So why don't we get taught or led through this process? Let's dive in to what it looks like.

THE ESSENTIAL ELEMENTS OF YOUR BACKSTORY

Your backstory is about so much more than your birth town. It's a combination of your:

FOUNDATIONS: all the fixed elements of your past like the neighborhood you grew up in, the siblings in your family, whether or not you had freckles or could run fast have influenced the path you're on. It's the DNA that makes you unique.

The foundations of your life are a fixed part of your backstory. You didn't choose to be born when you did or the family you were born with. You didn't get a say in being a big brother, or the middle sister, whether your skin was black or brown, if your parents were financially secure, if your dad told lame jokes or if your mom was a good cook.

Your backstory foundations set the course of your life. The time and place of your birth, your siblings (or lack thereof), the relationship of your parents, your ethnicity and culture, even the view of the world your family has was placed in your life for you to make sense of. Almost like water to a fish, you might not even notice the weight of impact your foundations have had on your life to this point.

CHARACTER: as a character in a story, what makes you unique, the parts of you that we could never guess based on what you look like or where you come from? It's the quirkiness of your personality, whether or not you grew up as a Star Wars fan, if you had a lot of friends growing up or just a couple of close ones.

You are the main character in the story of your life. In English class, we'd call you the protagonist. As the main character, a crucial part of understanding your story is to find out what makes you unique. You can be born into the same family as your siblings, have the same foundations, even be an identical twin, and still, you'd find a thousand ways that make you different.

Learning about the uniqueness of your character will help you understand everything about who you are. Your capacity for complexity, creativity, and empathy, your natural optimism, realism, and competitive nature are all unique to you. Even though you're with yourself all day long (ok, except maybe for the time you check out in class or at work, scroll through Instagram or play video games)- getting a complete grasp of who you are requires that you go through a process to examine each area.

MOMENTS: you've been through so much in your life, and it's all contributed to who you are. You've had redemptive moments, bitter moments, life-lesson moments, and more. Without taking the time to reflect on those pivotal moments, you'll never understand how they've shaped your life.

The moments of your life have shaped who you are and how you interact with the world. You've had pivotal moments, defining moments, and turning points. Some of them were unplanned, unexpected or even traumatic. Others were moments you hoped for, strived for, and hustled for.

The thing about moments is they happen to you, but you can easily miss their significance. You need to reflect on the moments you've had, to spend time processing what you went through, how it impacted you, how it stuck with you, and what changed. You need to allow yourself to remember, recall, and even feel what you need to feel for those moments to have the most resounding impact on your life. Sometimes, it's even necessary that you retell the details about those moments so that the painful emotions, even the way your body responds and remembers what happens, can be completed, integrated into your life, and transformed into something positive for your growth.

The memories of your significant moments need to be recalled, so you can understand them and make meaning from them.

FRAMES: whether or not they knew it, your family passed down the way they see everything in this world- family, friendship, work, money, and what it means to be a good neighbor. The frames you have for your life aren't fixed; they can be swapped out for more productive ones. But not until you figure out what they are.

You see life through particular lenses. It's not a bad thing, but you've been taught to view life's circumstances through different frames that likely confirm the biases that you already hold on to. If you have a frame that says people only look out for themselves, for example, then you'll likely see plenty of examples of people's selfish behavior to confirm your frame to be true. But if you have a frame that says all people are generally decent and kind, then you'll find no shortage of real-life examples of acts of kindness and generosity.

The thing about your frames is that they aren't fixed and can switch to different ones. You've been taught certain things about significant areas of life: family, money, work, time, spirituality, what it means to be a neighbor, and the meaning of friendship- and the first important step is to reflect on what you've learned. The second step, though, is to examine those frames to see what you think, to test them to see if they're productive for you, and then recognize you have the power to create your frames about life.

The frames you've created and been given about this life will shape everything you see and do.

Summary: If you reflect on each of the elements of your backstory, you'll be clear about where you come from and how it's shaped who you are. You can put them all together to more effectively answer the question, "Tell me about yourself." You will see more clearly where your life is going and how you might alter your trajectory. Other people will understand you better, leading to stronger connections. Can you imagine what you would miss if you didn't know your backstory?

Of course, the process of reflecting on your backstory isn't something that you do once and move on, it's a constant question that's open and changing throughout your life.

02: What makes you unique?
OWNING YOUR UNIQUE IDENTITY

I still remember a crucial moment during my middle school years that left scars on my self-esteem, probably until today, if I'm being honest. The NHL had just created a new hockey team in San Jose called the Sharks, and my dad had picked up a hat for me when he was near the new stadium. Even though I'm colorblind, I was stoked with the colors- kind of a teal bluish-green and black. All of my friends were wearing L.A. Kings hats (just like the music videos from Ice Cube and Dr. Dre), and I was going to be the one to stand out.

Unfortunately, I stood out too much- at least from one kid's perspective. It wasn't just any kid, this was THE kid on the bus who had catapulted into full-grown man size, complete with facial hair and pectoral muscles that the rest of us didn't have yet. It was likely powered by an extra dosage of testosterone which apparently also contributed to his aggressiveness that translated into a mild form of bullying and intimidation whenever he stepped foot on the bus.

Previously, he and I had no issues together. I steered clear and hadn't found my way into his crosshairs. But that morning, with my new hat, somehow when the bus stopped at school I inadvertently found myself right in front of him in the line to get out. He grabbed my hat, hard. He looked at it, laughed, and began showing it to the other kids around us.

"Look at this kid's hat- it's so stupid. I bet you don't even like this team, you just bought it for the colors. How freaking lame is this kid?"

At that moment, it was a middle schooler's worst nightmare- being made fun of and humiliated for something I thought would be cool and impressive. It was my absolute worst-case scenario- I was trying so hard to recover the confidence and popularity I had built in elementary school but, for some reason, couldn't elevate above the rest of the crowd and felt stuck as just a nobody. He was right (bullies usually are which is why they're so effective). I didn't like the team. I didn't even know a player on the team. I liked the colors. I wore it because I wanted people to notice me. I wanted to be different in a cool way.

Something happens inside adolescents starting around the age of 11 or 12. They become self-conscious and aware that they are real-life humans in a world of other humans. They become worried and anxious about being accepted and valued. They start looking at their peers as mirrors to understand their reflection. They yearn to be liked, approved of, and appreciated. Sadly, rarely do young teenagers get what they're looking for. Since everyone is on a similar quest, compliments, affirmation, and kindness are in short supply. Hardly anyone is willing to share the tiny shred of dignity or grace they carry as if it's a precious commodity.

There's nothing teenagers need more than acceptance, but the only way to be genuinely accepted is by being unique and different. It's ironic, isn't it? They fear rejection, so they go to great lengths to fit in, adapt, and blend in with the crowd. But then they lose themselves by trying to be like everyone else, leading to greater loneliness and isolation.

They need to be guided to a different conversation- to have the courage to reflect on what makes them unique, diverse, and memorable. They need a safe space to explore what makes them different and unique and drop the pursuit of trying to fit in for a little while.

I've learned over the years that I'm pretty quirky. For instance, I eat the same lunch every day and have since I was little. Every single day. At least if I can help it. Ham and swiss on sourdough with chips and an apple. That's it. I like to read biographies of historical figures. I own at least twenty golf putters and keep buying more. I take my dog for a walk at the same time on the same route every day.

I'm pretty quirky, but it's taken me a really long time to own it.

That's because, like everyone else, I want to fit in. On top of that, by default, my personality leads me to be highly adaptable and considerate of others- I want other people to feel cared for. Being super relational, I'm bent towards doing whatever makes you happy rather than declaring my desires. I'd rather listen to what you want to hear, set the thermostat to what you want, eat what you'd prefer to eat, and make sure you're happy.

But I've learned over the years that it's vital for me to get clear about what I want and declare it to the people in my life. Why? Because that's how relationships work. It's a back-and-forth. A give and take. When I withhold my preferences, I'm also withholding my true feelings, not being vulnerable. It's hard to have relationships of substance where one side is always giving.

Not only does owning my preferences make my relationships healthier and more robust, but it helps me make better decisions for my life, organize my work, and to make life more enjoyable.

I prefer to work last minute.
I prefer to do things on my own.
I prefer quick, direct feedback.
I prefer to do all the grocery shopping.
I prefer to have someone else proofread.

I prefer to work early in the morning.
I prefer the thermostat set to 73 degrees.

Your preferences aren't just about your favorite sauce for chicken nuggets (Chick-Fil-A sauce hands down) or your sleeping habits (always use white noise), it's also the preferences you have for learning, for working in teams, and for making decisions. Learning about your preferences and finding ways to communicate them as well as get what you need will make you stronger in all aspects.

The fact is this: There is no one like you. Never has been; never will be. No one will ever know what it's like to be you, think like you, see like you, act like you, or dream like you. No one will ever express themselves like you or make a mark like you. The world needs you to discover, own, and share the standout you.
What makes you unique and stand out?
There is beauty and wonder in all the differences, isn't there? There's no way we could all be alike- the world would be too predictable if we were. All the beauty, wonder, and creativity come through integrating the differences.
Fitting in is vital to a life well-lived. Belonging to others is key to feeling safe and nurtured. It's through others we experience and express love. Everyone needs safe, trusted people. Everyone needs a tribe. But relationships get funky when we don't respect the differences we bring. When we expect each other to see, think, feel, and act as we do- those are the ingredients of conflict and misunderstanding. When push comes to shove, though, most people will hide or mask or negate their uniqueness if it threatens a bond.
That's why it's so essential to discover, own, and express the standout you. We need each other to accept and appreciate the differences and see the differences in each other. We serve as mirrors of identity and

uniqueness; it's only by getting closer to people that we understand who we are and what makes us different.

We created a curriculum for students called The Standout You. It's a guided set of reflection exercises intended to facilitate self-awareness and confidence in who you are. The curriculum uses open-ended, reflective questions designed to spark thinking, curiosity, and insight. We encourage students to take every question a little deeper than they might usually. This isn't a curriculum to get through and complete; it's a journey to guide them to understand, own, and express themselves.

Like anything else in life, the more you put into it, the more you'll get out of it. Also, the more you share your responses and reflections with others, the better. The more you listen to other people respond to the same questions and prompts, the better. It's in the back- and-forth of sharing aloud that you're able to understand more, connect more dots, and see patterns. It's through sharing that you'll find the confidence to own and express what makes you standout.

In the course we guide students through a series of prompts and reflection questions relating to nine themes. Those nine themes are like lenses they look through into their lives that help them see what makes them distinctly unique. The proven process of prompted reflection questions, peer sharing, and conversations with adults will help students grow in self-awareness and confidence, and it's the foundation of a well-formed identity. Those themes are:

- **The Foundational You**: Your backstory foundations set the course of your life. The time and place of your birth, your siblings (or lack thereof), the relationship of your parents, your ethnicity and culture, even the view of the world your family has was placed in your life for you to make sense of. Almost like water to a fish, you might not even notice the weight of impact your foundations have had on your life to this point.

- **The Biological You**: You aren't a blank slate- you were born into a body with genes and DNA. You might not have spent much time thinking about it, but the biological you has shaped your life- how you act, how you feel, how others interact with you, and how you carry yourself. You might find some of these questions to be very personal or vulnerable. Unfortunately, in our culture we place a lot of importance on how we look. During the adolescent years, as our biology changes, it's especially important to regularly pause and reflect on how we're being shaped by the body we live in.
- **The Social You**: Nobody does it like you when it comes to friendships. You bring your humor, interests, quirks, values, and moral code. The ways you care, listen, encourage, and challenge are unique to you. That's what makes you such a valuable friend. Taking some time to reflect on who you are as it relates to relationships is essential to not only being the friend you want to be but also finding the friends you want to have.
- **The Philosophical You**: What you believe in, how you see the world, and the values, principles, and convictions you carry and express are a vital part of what makes you who you are. For many people, their philosophical foundations are abstract and unconscious. But, they drive everything you do and say. That's why it's so important to spend time reflecting on them and clarifying them. Every day you live, your new experiences, interactions, and connected ideas will build, change, or alter your philosophical beliefs.
- **The Experiential You**: The experiences you've been through have shaped your outlook, perspective, and attitude. Each experience you go through stays with you, and your brain naturally seeks ways to make sense of it. No one else has

experienced what you have; no one interprets your shared experiences the same way. Without realizing it, you might make meaning out of your experiences that doesn't serve you or help you flourish. That's why it's critical to recall and reflect on your experiences. You always have the opportunity to change your interpretation, to rewrite the story.

- **The Creative You**: You were created to be creative. You came out of the womb that way. Whether it was stacking blocks, attaching Legos, singing, dancing, or selling cookies, the unique viewpoint, style, and connections you make as a creative are like a fingerprint to you. Learning to reflect on your creative style, natural abilities, and motivations will help you realize your unique identity and find the confidence you need to keep creating. The world needs you to embrace your identity as a creative fully.

- **The Working You**: How you approach work, whether schoolwork, chores like folding laundry, or an actual 9–5 job, says a lot about who you are. The teen years are challenging when it comes to work- you are given assignments and tasks whether or not you want them, and your compensation varies and is not guaranteed. However, this is a critical time to understand yourself better and make decisions about how you will approach work for the rest of your life.

- **The Preferential You**: Where are you going? What will you do? What kind of person will you turn into? There's no one else like you- not now, and not then. Learning to take time to think about your future, dream even, will help you grow more aware of the uniqueness of the path that you're on. Even if you choose a role model to emulate, the way you go down that path and the person you become will have its own unique expression.

- **The Quirky You**: You aren't just unique; you're weird. Not in a wrong way- just a quirky way. Put ketchup on scrambled eggs?

Always jump over the cracks in the sidewalk? Chew your toenails? Pronounce Wed-nes-day? Talk to your plants? Yeah, we've all got them. Quirks, idiosyncrasies, and bizarre rituals. They're a part of what makes you unique and delightful. Odd? Yep. Annoying? Perhaps. Authentic? You betcha. Reflecting on your quirks is one step towards becoming more self-aware and more self-confident. Be you- everyone else is already taken.

The final exercise is a presentation project, whether in written, video, audio, or a public speaking medium, where each student answers the ultimate question with clarity:

What makes you stand out?

When students have an opportunity to process their identity and share what makes them unique in the company of peers, they can receive the mirroring and affirmation everyone needs to form a secure identity. That's the foundation for wellbeing and it becomes a critical part of a life compass to know how to navigate through complexity.

Summary: Discovering, owning, and expressing the unique attributes of who you are is critical to constructing a meaningful life. It gives you more confidence in yourself and what makes you different from others, in a healthy way. It leads to self-acceptance and self-esteem, which are foundational ingredients to resilience and appropriate risk-taking. You will have the clarity to say yes to opportunities and offers that are congruent with who you are, and the courage to say no when it would lead you elsewhere. Can you imagine what you'd miss out on if you didn't own your unique identity?

03 What do you stand for?
DEFINING YOUR FUNDAMENTAL VALUES

Most of the time Popeye was a big pushover. Maybe he felt like he had to be — who dresses like that, anyway? But when push came to shove (literally), he always rolled up his sleeves and got into the fight. Can you remember his catchphrase? It was:

"That's all I can stands, cause I can't stands no more!"

What do you stand for? What are you willing to roll up your sleeves and get into the fight for?

Those are foundational questions that form the basis for your fundamental values- the issues and aspects of life that are so important to you they motivate the core of everything you do, see, and say. Do you know what your fundamental values are? The things that drive you, fuel you, irritate you and inspire you?

Recently, my son and I talked about his transition to high school and how different the rigor of academics will be compared to middle school. He asked me if I thought it was important for him to get good grades and try hard to do well in school. I told him he might not care right now about getting good grades, but three years from now, when it's time to apply for college, the 12th-grade version of himself would appreciate the 9th-grade version putting his total effort into doing well. I was trying to tell him he wanted options for if and where to go to college. His response: *"How am I supposed to know what to do with my life- I'm only 15!"*

He's far from the first kid to convey that sentiment. Every teenager feels the pressure to figure themselves out and pick a path in life. Why? For one, every adult in their life will ask that question constantly. Also, kids are aware of the pressure to figure out a life for themselves, and, as they will eventually realize, living at the beach is expensive. Six months ago, my son was 100% committed to mountain biking. A year before that? Baseball. Currently, it's all about surfing. How could he possibly imagine where his interests and passion will be three years from now- not to mention a decade?

That's why it's rarely helpful for a kid to pick a career or academic path based on interests alone. Or on where the jobs are going to be. Or based on average salary. Or based on what you're strongest in academically.

What's most important is doing the work to define what's most important to you. To determine your fundamental values, the things that you stand for at your core.

Although those are influenced by your family and community and cultural perspective, fundamental values can only be defined and declared by the individual. They have to come from within.

Most people find clarity in their fundamental values by looking into their backstory and discovering something they lacked. You might hear someone say: "I really care about kids who don't have father figures because I didn't have a father figure," or, "I'm all about helping women understand how worthy they are because I didn't get that message when I was growing up." Sometimes what we didn't receive becomes a core driver for us. Or you might have had an exceptional, uncommon experience that shaped you positively and realize most people don't receive what you did, so you want to share that with them.

Growing up, I wasn't bullied, but I was often overlooked. Whether it was because of my shy personality or my social anxiety to put myself out there, my experience caused me to feel forgotten and lacking value. The older I got and the more confident I became in myself, I realized that I have a sensitive radar to social situations where someone feels excluded. I can feel it acutely when someone comes into a room yet isn't greeted. When a group of people forms a circle, it physically blocks someone from participating. I do more than just cringe; I intervene and sometimes get angry. I just can't stand the thought of someone else feeling what I felt so often.

Now, not so ironically, I focus my professional attention on helping people find their value by reflecting on their unique stories. I created a job where I help people feel seen and known, and appreciated in their uniqueness. I've taken a fundamental value and translated it directly into my professional life.

The thing is, without understanding what you stand for, it's hard to know how to organize your life. It's confusing to know what to fight for. It's hard to find clarity about what to do with your life- how to spend your energy, your time, where to invest your learning, or what to do with your creativity.

Students decide who they are, and where they're headed in their lives during middle and high school. They deserve an opportunity to reflect and find clarity on their most essential values- to process them in writing and conversation. We need to challenge students to explain them, share where they come from, why they're so vital to them, and present how they've used their values to decide what to do.

Here are a few prompts to help clarify your fundamental values:

- *What did you not receive in your childhood that impacted your life negatively? What would be different if you had received it?*
- *What did you receive in your childhood that impacted your life positively?*
  If other people received what you did, how would it affect them?
- *Finish this sentence: Everyone deserves…because…*
- *Finish this sentence: What ticks me off is…because…*
- *What do your responses to those prompts say about what's most important to you?*
- *What do you stand for? What are you willing to fight for? Why?*

There's a collective theory in the world that tells young people they can't figure themselves out. They have to wait until they get older. But that's not true! We just don't have self-awareness as a goal or an expectation for students when they graduate high school…yet.

If you work with students or are a parent, one of the most important things you can do is share your fundamental values and where they come from. They need to see someone older than them share about what drives them and reflect on what led them there. It's hard to change course in your life when you've already started down a path. It's a lot more effective if you figure out where you're going ahead of time- so you can avoid detours and wasted time.

They need to be constantly reminded of a simple message: This is your life, don't let anyone else write your story.

Summary: It's interesting- we ask students how to write clear, persuasive essays and perform the Pythagorean theorem, but don't quiz them on what's most important to them. Which has more lasting, relevant value for their future? Of course, values are more caught than taught, but the critical translation to make other people's values your own comes after you think through them and express them in your own words. Can you imagine what someone would miss out on if they didn't define their fundamental values?

04 What do you believe in?
DEFINING YOUR FUNDAMENTAL BELIEFS

I didn't grow up with any beliefs, or so I thought. From a religious or spiritual perspective, our family didn't align with them. We weren't overly patriotic; we didn't study philosophy, and there was no family motto besides a few funny phrases my grandpa would say.

When I got to college, I was dating a girl who went to a devout Christian university down the road from where I was studying. I spent time with her friends, who were mandated to attend chapel services three times a week. They would talk about the chapel topics, usually stories and characters from the Bible when we'd hang out. I had no idea what they were talking about, having never cracked open a Bible once in my life. Suddenly, I felt insecure about my family's lack of religious certitude or affiliation.

We didn't have any stated creeds or theology- but we had clearly formed beliefs. We believed in putting our family first. We believed in service to others. We believed in hard work paying off, trying our hardest in every situation, and that we could fix any problem given enough determination. It took me years to realize that not only did I come from a firm foundation of beliefs, but they continued to propel my life and undergird everything I did.

What you believe shapes who you become. Your beliefs shape how you see the world and how you interact with it. They form the foundation of your identity, how you understand your purpose and interact with the world, and the quality of relationships you build.

Not only do we all have foundational beliefs about how the world works, but we also have the opportunity as we grow up to find and align ourselves with a larger story. This overarching belief can both organize our lives and fuel us to grow, learn, and contribute. Whether you find that story through a religious framework or not, the benefits are the same- you implicitly know that your life matters, you have something to contribute, and the world needs you. In other words, life is not about you. It's not about your comfort or preferences; it's about giving yourself to a more significant cause.

When students (or anyone) lose sight of something big to believe in- it affects everything. It impacts their mental health, motivation to work hard in school, ability to make healthy choices, and hope for the future. Schools work so hard to promote self-directed learning and motivation through instructional practices, but they forget the greater human need to find an overarching worldview.

Parents, families, and communities do their best to pass on their beliefs to the next generation. Through wisdom that comes with age and life experience, they want the next generation to see the world in similar ways. **But the question is: how do you effectively pass on your beliefs?**

It starts with knowing which questions to ask. It can feel counterintuitive, though. Most parents and teachers will default to a lecture format. They feel anxious about kids getting beliefs 'wrong', so they lecture, cajole, and sometimes threaten. However, in my experience, teenagers need a safe environment to explore views independently. They need an opportunity to test out 'wrong beliefs' for themselves, without fear of the adults in their life getting mad at them.

It's almost as though any attempt to force your beliefs on the next generation guarantees the opposite: rebellion.

Here are a few prompts to help students (and you) clarify your core beliefs:
- *Do you believe the world is basically a friendly place or is it dangerous, uncontrollable, and up to you to get through it?*
- *Do you believe that you are in charge of creating your future, or are you subject to however things shake out?*
- *Do you believe you have inherent potential, or is it more what-you-see-is-what-you-get?*
- *Do you believe in God, and if so, what kind of God? Is He for you? Is He available? Does He have a power that can be tapped into on your behalf?*

If you work with students or are a parent, it's critical for you to share with them what your core beliefs are and where they come from. Students need challenging opportunities to define their own beliefs and what they mean. These are questions we CAN expect them to answer by the time they graduate and move into the world on their own if we expect them to.

Eventually, I did find a religious framework that resonated with me. For the past twenty years, it's informed my decisions and shaped my work in the world. I've also learned to integrate that system with the foundation I grew up with. In times of uncertainty or crisis, my beliefs have given me clarity and strength to make wise choices. That's something we want for every kid growing up.

Summary: everyone has beliefs, even if they don't consider themselves religious. Beliefs are formed unconsciously through our family of origin and life experiences. Sometimes, we have beliefs that won't lead us to a flourishing life. Sometimes, we have beliefs that are inconsistent with our values. Everyone needs to reflect on their own beliefs, to scrutinize and examine them. If they don't work for you or are incongruent with your values, look for different beliefs. Can you imagine what someone would miss out on if they didn't have clearly defined fundamental beliefs?

05 What have you been healed from?
DEALING WITH UNRESOLVED EXPERIENCES

Everyone has challenges that impede their growth and development. We all have villains in our life stories who oppose us and keep us from becoming who we're meant to become. Sometimes those villains are people, sometimes they're life experiences or tragic moments, and sometimes they're roadblocks or setbacks.

Some of those blips in our life stories turn into ongoing challenges and problems to face. We carry them with us, and often without realizing it those villains continue to attack, haunt, or plague us.

- *For the kid who got bullied in middle school, who freezes anytime someone at work 'powers up' and uses a loud voice.*
- *For the kid who had their heart broken in high school, and still pushes loved ones away subconsciously.*

- *For the kid who missed the shot, with groans from the stands and turned backs from teammates, who now gets extremely anxious before giving big presentations at work.*

Call those scenarios traumatic? Maybe. Did it affect us throughout our lives? Yes.

It's hard to go through life without experiencing trauma, especially if you hold a broad definition of what trauma means. The research on Adverse Childhood Experiences has opened our understanding of how kids respond to painful and traumatic experiences. If we don't acknowledge the trauma, reflect on it, process it productively through guided support, and receive validation from people we trust, we are likely to stay stuck in the adverse effects of trauma:

> "Each age group is vulnerable in unique ways to the stresses of a disaster, with children and the elderly at greatest risk. Young children may display generalized fear, nightmares, heightened arousal and confusion, and physical symptoms, (e.g., stomachaches, headaches). School-age children may exhibit symptoms such as aggressive behavior and anger, regression to the behavior seen at younger ages, repetitious traumatic play, loss of ability to concentrate, and worse school performance. Adolescents may display depression and social withdrawal, rebellion, increased risky activities such as sexual acting out, wish for revenge and action-oriented responses to trauma, and sleep and eating disturbances." (<u>Trauma-Informed Care in Behavioral Health Services</u>)

Unprocessed trauma hinders learning; it erodes healthy adult development and maturity and can ruin someone's life. Having worked closely with hundreds of transitioning veterans for the past six years, especially those who served in special forces, I'm aware of how unprocessed trauma can prevent someone from flourishing in a meaningful life. We tell students, educators, and parents the same thing we say to veterans:

It's hard to build a flourishing life on top of one that's still hurt or broken.

Thankfully, Trauma-Informed Care (aka Trauma-Informed Practice) is a recent area of focus within social services including K-12 education. It's an attempt to recognize unprocessed trauma in students' lives and provide a framework for providers or educators to adjust their work with people to accommodate for unresolved trauma. The key message is that trauma is present in the classroom and needs to be addressed. Teachers need to put the social and emotional needs in front of instructional goals or outcomes- or else you'll never reach the goals.

The hopeful message is that we can help kids process the trauma inside them and keep them stuck. We can put kids first, we can adapt to their needs, we can be more flexible in our classroom management and lesson plans- but it requires a change in priority and a beginner's mind. It requires a refreshed understanding of what success looks like to educate kids and prepare them to flourish in life.

One teacher recently reacted strongly to me in response to that idea. He said, "You're asking me to do something I'm not equipped to do- I'm not trained to be a school psychologist." I responded immediately: "Oh no- not at all. Psychologists are trained to diagnose disorders and psychological problems and prescribe effective solutions- and you're not trained for that. I'm asking you to consider being inquisitive about your students' personal lives. I'm asking you to make it a priority to guide them into opportunities to reflect on their lives and what they've been through and share those experiences through writing and in conversation with peers. Because I know you care for kids, I know you're passionate about what they learn- and you can either implement these strategies now or deal with them later."

Every student deserves an opportunity to build a meaningful life. In our work to build a foundation for them to flourish, we need to learn about trauma; we need to go first in resolving our unprocessed trauma, and we need to guide students to process theirs. Without that, they will always struggle to thrive.

I'll never forget a beautiful conversation I was a part of with a small group of student leaders a few years ago. We'd worked through a long twelve-week curriculum together, our LifeScript course that prompts them to reflect on the story of their lives. Throughout two dozen class periods, we took turns sharing stories and talking aloud about the moments and experiences that shaped us. At the last class together, a few days before graduation, I asked them to reflect on the experience of going through the curriculum together. What it sparked was nothing short of a divine moment.

One student shared something she hadn't revealed before, a secret she was holding onto. Two years earlier, she took an extended leave of absence from school but never explained where she went or what happened. Kids had just assumed she was sick at home. Instead, she confessed that she had gotten to a bad place with an eating disorder, and her parents checked her into an inpatient care facility. The other students in our class responded with grace and kindness, one student hugging her and whispering how much she loved her.

Another student confronted a member of our group and said, "Remember when we weren't friends for like three years?" The boy said, "Yeah- what was that all about? All of a sudden, you stopped talking to me and ignored me." She responded, *"You know why-* you were dating my best friend and cheated on her at Homecoming." Flushed with emotion, he looked at her and then said, "Yeah- I was such an idiot. Honestly. I wish I could go back in time and change things. I made a mistake, and I'm so sorry." With tears in both of their eyes, she said, "Well, you're forgiven. And I'm glad we're friends now."

In that short moment, students were processing through significant, painful things they'd been through BEFORE they graduated from high school. Are you kidding me? Most of us never have the chance. We anxiously walk into the side door of our twenty-year high school reunion, still carrying the residue of mistakes, shame, guilt, or humiliation that's never been adequately addressed.

What if we allowed students to appropriately deal with the junk we all go through before they build an adult life? It's tough to make a thriving, happy life when you're carrying guilt, trauma, grief, or pain.

What have you learned about villains or trauma in your own life, and how are you helping those you serve to deal with theirs?

Summary: no one escapes painful experiences; they're a part of life. Many people, however, lack the tools to resolve the residue from trauma. They just don't know how to work through it productively, so they carry it with them into other aspects of their life, unaware their lens has been tainted. They continue to brace themselves, calling upon survival instincts when they find themselves in situations that don't require them. No one escapes painful experiences, but we all deserve an opportunity to work through them, learn from them, and grow from them. Can you imagine a life well-lived when you're still captured by trauma?

06 What do you struggle with?
OWNING AND MANAGING YOUR WEAKNESSES

I have a friend who claims to be terrible at math. She says it was her worst subject, and now that she has kids, she freaks out that her kids are going to have problems on their homework that she can't help solve. But here's the relevant question: how does she know that she's terrible at math?

It's not just with math, but pick any weakness you have. How do you know it's a weakness? When did you first notice it? Who told you it was a weakness? Why is it a weakness for you?

I've asked her these kinds of questions about her lack of weakness in math, and she really didn't know the answers to any of those questions. She just knows that math was always a struggle, she never really understood it, and her grades reflected that.

But what if?

What if she wasn't naturally bad at math like she's assumed her entire adult life? What if there was a different problem, a problem that started at the beginning?

What if, on the first day of her first Algebra class in Middle School, she was assigned a seat in the back, next to the class clown? The kid who made it his life's goal to distract everyone around him and not care about school, like him. Or what if her first Algebra teacher was new to teaching, and hadn't quite mastered the fundamentals of explaining complex math concepts to pre-teens? Math is one of those subjects that tends to build over time, so what if she missed the foundational concepts? It's no wonder she struggled in Algebra 2, Pre-Calculus, and certainly College Math! What if her attitude has always been terrible towards math, and her work ethic and desire to dig into the challenges kept her constantly swimming upstream? Besides a blanket assumption that she lacks the innate ability, there could be so many other variables at play.

When you identify a weakness, it deserves more than just a write-off. Your weaknesses deserve an opportunity to be explored, understood, and resolved.

There's always more to the story when it comes to your weaknesses. Sure, you don't want to be hindered by them. Your weaknesses drag you down and limit your potential and productivity. But, too often, we neglect to explore our weaknesses because they bring up big feelings inside of us, big, uncomfortable feelings.

For some, they avoid their weaknesses at all costs. They don't want to talk about them, think about them, or address them. Having other people point them out is the worst. They want to keep a pristine image of themselves, sometimes at any cost.

For others, they spend too much time there. Maybe they absorbed a message growing up about how their weaknesses form the majority of their identity. In other words, they have a negative self-image, and their struggle is not about recognizing their shortcomings, but about owning any positive strengths.

In reality, given an environment of psychological safety and empathetic, kind people, exploring your weaknesses might be the start of tremendous growth and change. As Michael Jordan once famously said, "My attitude is that if you push me towards something that you think is a weakness, then I will turn that perceived weakness into a strength." With humility and a little Mamba mentality (Kobe!), finding out about a weakness might be the nudge you need to get in gear. At the very least, it will help you become more aware of who you are, and who you're not. Imagine how many people you know started down a path in life to live up to someone else's expectations for them.

Growing up, I had significant speech delays. Not only did it make it more stressful for me to form words and sentences when I was little, but I developed a habit of being a listener more than a talker. Throughout the years, the critique or snide comment I would hear would be about me being too quiet, too shy, or too mysterious. When it came time for me to talk in class or give a presentation, I would especially freeze up. But I kept working at it. I forced myself into social situations. I made commitments to myself to raise my hand in class at least once. Later in college, I joined a leadership club and forced myself to share my ideas. I would even write them down ahead of time to prepare to talk. Eventually, I was invited to speak in front of a larger audience. It was just to give a brief announcement about an upcoming event, but, as it turned out, I was really good at it. It's almost like all of that listening and focus I had done for so many years translated into thoughtful clarity when I spoke. Friends and peers shared unsolicited compliments about me speaking up front, and I was hooked. Twenty years later, I am a professional speaker and have provided for my family through what was my major weakness for the first half of my life.

Young people are deciding about their identity that will shape their future. We can help them explore their weaknesses to understand them and resolve them and figure out what options they have to manage them. Sometimes, you ought to avoid weaknesses at all costs. Sometimes, you need to hire a tutor. Sometimes, you need to change your attitude.

We don't need to worry when we explore our weaknesses. With honesty and humility, exploring our weaknesses can be instructive about our identity. In coming to a better understanding of them, we can figure out what to do with them. And, who knows, in facing our weaknesses, they just might grow into resilient and wise adults.

There's always more to the story of your weaknesses. Sure, you don't want to be hindered by them. Your weaknesses drag you down and limit your potential and productivity. But, too often, we neglect to explore our weaknesses because they bring up big feelings inside of us, big, uncomfortable feelings.

But, learning to embrace our weaknesses and challenges can be really helpful. For one, we can realize that weakness gets in our way to something important to us, then do what we need to do to overcome that weakness. Also, if you embrace a weakness, you might realize that it would be better just to avoid that thing altogether. No use trying if it's never going to work, right?

Embracing a weakness can also lead us to lean on other people. Since we're all wired differently, there are probably people already in your life who are naturally wired to be good at something you're not. That's one of the beautiful parts of friendship and community- we can learn to lean on each other in a mutually beneficial way.

Summary: Understanding what you struggle with and how to manage your weaknesses is critical to building the foundation for a meaningful life. Everyone has an opportunity to decide what to do with their weaknesses- whether to avoid them, hide from them, be haunted by them, or confess them. We need to decide if we want to turn a weakness into a strength, or hire someone else to manage it for us. We need self-awareness and courage to confront them, leading to growth and humility. Can you imagine a life well-lived if you never learn what your weaknesses are or what to do about them?

07 What has failure taught you?
LESSONS FROM FAILURE

I can't stand failing- it's the worst. I try so hard to avoid it at all costs. The most painful memories of my past are about failure. Getting cut from the team, getting caught cheating on a test, cheating on a girlfriend, and getting fired (several times) are all stops on my personal walk of shame.

Maybe you'd be surprised to hear me say this: I'm so thankful I went through those failures.

Failure taught me a lot about myself, my values, and about persistence. It helped me look in the mirror and ask myself tough questions about who I am and who I want to be. It freed me from a few obligations that, in hindsight, I was stuck in.

There's not a failure I can remember where I didn't grow immensely because of it- mostly because I had people in my life who supported me. My mom was a key figure to guide me through my failures- she always would tell me the truth yet hold me in acceptance and grace. My wife has done the same. I've had friends along the way who've picked me up and helped me process what I went through.

Having a supportive guide is critical to help us learn from our failures.

A guide's role is to come alongside someone to help them interpret reality and see clearly. Everyone needs a guide; kids especially. A guide will ask probing questions and be an accurate, honest mirror.

There are two aspects of our culture that concern me when it comes to failure:

1. **Image Management** Our world has tipped heavily towards image management. The message is: "You are what others think about you." Maintain a positive image at all costs. Sure, we can blame social media and extremely competitive college admissions- they perpetuate the idea that we're only as good as our brand.

2. **Protection Parenting** We also have to look in the mirror at our own parenting. We don't want our kids to feel the discomfort of failure, so we protect them, prevent them, and knockdown obstacles for them. We don't hold them accountable- we blame teachers, district policies, coaches, or 'other groups' of people.

If we don't let kids fail, they won't learn significant truths about life.

They won't learn about persistence. They won't be able to discern what's most important. They won't be able to learn that their true worth comes from within, not from their reputation. They won't learn that they can handle hard things, and they will be predisposed to avoid taking risks.

Inability to face, accept, or learn from failure is one of the most consistent critiques managers in today's workplace have about the younger generations. Just the other day I was talking with two managers of a large global company who lamented how few risks their team members were willing to take. Whether it was speaking up in meetings or coming up with new initiatives, they consistently held back. One of them shared how she'd given honest feedback to a young employee, who instantly broke down crying and claimed she was being treated in a hostile manner.

Life is going to be hard. No one's going to escape setbacks, obstacles, or failure. If you do, it's likely because you're taking the path of least resistance and avoiding anything that might be uncomfortable. The workplace needs emerging talent to embrace and continuously lean into failure. There's no better time to teach them this valuable life lesson than during adolescence.

Failing sucks, right? Especially when it's public and other people know about it. Whether it's missing the shot to lose the game, failing the test, getting busted for cheating, most of us try to avoid failure at all costs. A lot of times, our parents protect us from failing. They don't want us to feel bad or to miss out.

Once you learn to appreciate failure, the next time you're freer to take the next shot, to bounce back from the D- grade you got and go to office hours, and to own your mistakes to do better.

Summary: A key foundational element for being prepared to build a meaningful life is learning from failure, and the willingness to take risks even if it means you might fail again. Can you imagine someone who runs from failure, and still living well? Can you imagine someone living a well-lived life and never confronting the pain they feel from past failures?

08 What challenges or setbacks have you pushed through?
DEMONSTRATIONS OF RESILIENCE

Life is hard for everyone. There's no escaping setbacks, failure, or disappointment. Some people get dealt a more difficult hand, but everyone has bad things happen to them.

How much more for people who want to do something great with their lives.

A lot has been written over the past decade about helicopter parents. Now, lawnmower parents are all the craze- the parents who "go to whatever lengths necessary to prevent their child from having to face adversity, struggle, or failure." But we're trying to prepare kids for more than a comfortable life. We want more for them than happiness, success, or fulfillment even. We want them to be equipped to build a meaningful life. And a meaningful life will be a difficult road.

Growing up, I struggled with significant developmental and speech delays. I went to occupational and speech therapy for years and I remember how embarrassed I felt when I got pulled out of class each week. Physically, I had challenges, too- I broke nine bones over the years. The worst blow was breaking my knee the night before my Little League baseball season started. I had just made the team and worked hard for a year to get a starting position at 3rd base. It crushed me.

Those experiences became a part of my story, especially because I would listen to my mom tell people about my experiences. I can remember her talking to friends on the phone about how courageous and strong I was. I would listen as she commented about how impressed she was with how I could handle hard things. That feedback built confidence in me that I could handle the next hard thing.

Years later, I reached a crossroads to go down the path of comfort in a career in accounting or take the riskier path of working with students for a non-profit. I chose the narrow road. I've watched many friends over the years choose the comfortable path because they felt anxious about the hardships and challenges. I've had colleagues pull the cord and go into a more stable and comfortable industry. I've had partners in this entrepreneurial journey who would get overwhelmed by the trials of this unpredictable lifestyle.

But every time I hit a roadblock, I take a step back and recall all the hard things I've been through in my life, personally and professionally. I know I can face this challenge because I've faced so many before. In fact, this new challenge will build even greater strength and determination in me, because I know I will get through it.

Carol Dweck has helped popularize the concept of a growth mindset compared to a fixed one (if you don't want to read the entire book, watch her famous TED talk from 2014). We can help kids cultivate their responses to challenges, whether those challenges are about learning a new math concept or a swim stroke, or making new friends. Kids create frames to experience and see life through from the adults in their lives, and how we respond to the challenges they face influences their interpretations. As we consider our own mindset towards challenges and cultivate an attitude of acceptance, gratitude, and reflection, we can both model resilience and guide students to develop a similar one.

Kids need multiple opportunities to "feel, fail, and fall" in their lives, as parenting expert author Shefali Tsabury puts it. That's how they learn about life and how the world works, about who they are, and about how to navigate through life effectively. The more opportunities kids have to face setbacks, failure, and disappointments with caring, non-anxious adults close to them- the more they will have the muscle mass and muscle memory to grow. We can carve out multiple opportunities at home and throughout the school day to guide students to reflect on the challenges they're facing, to think about how they're responding to those challenges, and reflect on alternative options that would be more productive for building the foundations for a flourishing life.

There's nothing worse than wanting something and finding out you can't get it yet. It's so, so tempting to just give up. Maybe you tried out for a team but got the news that you wouldn't make the squad this year, but the coach encouraged you to keep training. Maybe you auditioned for a leading part but got Tree #2. Or maybe you really wanted to get an A in the midterm but struggled to get a C+.

Grit is a mixture of your passion and your persistence. It's a long commitment to learning a skill, accomplishing a goal, or gaining an attribute- no matter what it takes or how long it takes.

Hopefully, you've had the opportunity by now to earn some grit. Hopefully, you know what it's like to dig deep and pursue something, even if it's hard or takes a while. But even if you haven't yet, don't worry- there's still time.

- *What's something you wanted but didn't get at first? What did you do to persevere?*
- *What's something you want now, but it's not attainable to you yet? What will you do to keep striving?*
- *Who's someone you look up to, whether you know them personally, who shows grit? In what way?*
- *What would it do for your life if you grew in grit? What could be possible?*

If you've been alive for more than a day, then you know things don't always go your way. If you've gone to school for a day, you know that's true. Other people set your schedule. Other people tell you what to eat, what you can't wear, what you shouldn't say, what you need to do next. And, sometimes, there are things you want to happen in your life and the door gets closed.

- *What's your default response when things don't go your way?*

In life, you're going to face a lot of resistance, especially if you seek to pursue a life of big ambitions and goals. That resistance might be external- a barrier, a person, resources, or qualifications. Or, it might be internal- insecurity, fear, or doubt.

I'm so grateful I've had an adult in my life helping me interpret and reflect the truth during my challenges over the years. My mom has helped me not only know that 'this too shall pass' but also to know that I will become stronger if I face it.

Summary: A key foundational element for being prepared to build a meaningful life is the experience of pushing through setbacks and still prevailing. Setbacks are a part of life- no one can avoid them. In the context of a story, it's the setbacks that make it worth watching or reading or listening to. The conflicts we face are what shapes our character and predict our path in life. Can you imagine what someone would miss out on if they avoided setbacks?

09 How do you learn best?
UNDERSTANDING YOUR LEARNING STYLE

Unless a kid has been assessed for unique learning challenges or disabilities, they will have to survive in a one-size-fits-all model of learning. Good teachers will employ strategies to provide differentiated learning plans within a classroom using scaffolding techniques. They know students have different learning styles, and they do the best they can to offer the resources to adapt to those differences.

But with large class sizes, fast-paced trimesters, a focus on testing, and ultra-competitive college admissions, not every student will get the opportunity to develop a love for learning, an awareness of their learning style, or have the time to pursue their curiosity.

That's a shame, to say the least. If you can't cope with the system, you'll get left behind. If you can't hack it, you'll feel like something's wrong with you.

Valerie Strauss, director of the scathing documentary **The Race to Nowhere**, talks about the unintended consequences of focusing exclusively on performance on test scores in a Washington Post article: "Even for those students who stick with it, tests degrade the educational experience, fueling performance anxiety and the false impression that academic success is about speed, accuracy and competition." For all the emphasis on testing, there are millions of kids who are being left behind, and millions more who meet the educational requirements but are missing out on actual learning.

Sir Ken Robinson (R.I.P.!) famously said in one of his TED talks, "The dropout crisis is just the tip of an iceberg. What it doesn't count are all the kids who are in school but are disengaged from it, who don't enjoy it, who don't get any real benefit from it."

So what can we do, as adults involved in the education of kids?

Teachers, keep working on those differentiation and scaffolding skills.

Parents, be diligent to notice where your kid's curiosity is pointing. Encourage them to learn more, provide resources for them if appropriate (sign them up for a class, a digital course, or connect them with an industry practitioner).

Teachers and Parents, ask open-ended reflection questions about their learning (and expect your students to respond). Questions to help them become more self-aware, like:

- *When do you learn best? What environment?*
- *What's most distracting to you when you're doing schoolwork?*
- *What helps you learn better? What do your favorite teachers do?*
- *What tricks or hacks have you found to help you stay on top of your work?*
- *What are you learning that will be useful in your life later on?*
- *What's most interesting to you right now about what you're learning?*
- *Why do you think you're learning this right now?*

We want students to be inherently curious, self-aware, and self-driven. We want them to know why they're learning, not just become proficient at school. It's going to take some thoughtful reflection and the willingness on our part to take an alternative route.

Not to mention the courage to give them permission to be themselves...

We all learn differently- some visually, some by using our hands, and some by being told. Unfortunately, we don't all get personalized learning plans, tailor made to our natural abilities or predispositions. On top of that, one of the most common criticisms of the way the school system is set up is that it requires you to memorize facts and information, rather than truly learn. What good is it if you know when the War of 1812 started, but you don't understand why two countries with drastically different worldviews would grapple over a small rock in the middle of an ocean?

Learning is what matters, and since we all learn differently, it's important to become aware of how you learn best. We can't depend on teachers or parents to spoon-feed us just the way we want. Someday, our bosses will require us to learn without any hand holding. Someday you might commit yourself to a cause and be a part of solving an important problem, but there's going to be no one there to tutor you- you're going to have to figure it out yourself.

When push comes to shove, and it's really important, how do you learn best?

For one, there are actual assessments that can help you understand your learning style (check out the Multiple Intelligences one). Also, it's helpful to do some self-reflection, to make some observations about yourself so you can better understand your learning style. It really helps to watch and listen to how other people learn best- either you might find that you resonate with their style, or they serve as an upside-down mirror, and you can see what makes you different from them.

- When you have to figure something out, where do you turn? Do you tend to ask a friend, spend time searching on the internet, experimenting yourself, or find someone to show you?
- What's the best way for you to study for a test? WIth a friend or a small group? By yourself? Have someone ask you questions?
- What's the best way for you to figure out how something works when it's broken? Look for how-to videos, play around with it yourself, or get someone to walk you through it step-by-step?
- If you had to become an expert at a topic, how would you do it?

Summary: A key foundational element for being prepared to build a meaningful life is the knowledge of your personal learning style and the ability to manage your life to get what you need to learn best. Since everyone learns differently, we all need to understand our unique style. We can't assume or expect other people- teachers or bosses, to cultivate the perfect plan for us. It's our life, learning is up to us. Can you imagine what you'd miss out on if you never understood your preferred learning style and made adjustments?

10 What have you learned about yourself?
ACCURATE SELF–AWARENESS

One of the bizarre aspects of parenting that no one prepares you for is watching the same movies again and again and again and again until every line is memorized. Most of the time, it's mind-numbing to watch the film the first time, much less the ninth time. But every now and then my kids fall in love with a film that captures my heart, too.

Disney's Tangled is the animated story of Rapunzel- based loosely on the German fairy tale by the Brothers Grimm. In the original story, Rapunzel is sought after by a prince. In Disney's version, Rapunzel is ignited to go on her own exploration of self-discovery, to explore who she is and where she comes from. She intuitively knows that there's more to herself than she's been told, and enlists a boy-bandit named Flynn Rider to guide her. The rest of the movie is about Rapunzel's journey to discover where she came from and who she really is.

Daniel Goleman is the godfather of learning about yourself, especially as it relates to management and organizational health. He said, "If your emotional abilities aren't in hand, if you don't have self-awareness, if you are not able to manage your distressing emotions, if you can't have empathy and have effective relationships, then no matter how smart you are, you are not going to get very far." Coining the term EQ (Emotional Intelligence), Goleman almost single-handedly changed the public perception about self-discovery, and the management industry has jumped on his bandwagon. Harvard Professor of Cognition and Education Howard Gardner said, "The less a person understands his own feelings, the more he will fall prey to them. The less a person understands the feelings, the responses, and the behavior of others, the more likely he will interact inappropriately with them and therefore fail to secure his proper place in the world." It's become normal to get to know yourself.

But, the self-discovery journey is a long one. Despite its accepted value, most people have never taken the opportunity to explore the insides of who they are, where they've come from, or how they come across to others. It's complex, overwhelming, and takes a really long time and a lot of energy. The journey doesn't really have an end. And there are haters every step of the way. People convincing you to quit being so "self-consumed". People's eyes glazing over when you start talking about the deeper parts of you. Derogatory names like "navel-glazer" or narcissist.

Like Rapunzel, though, I think there's something deep inside all of us that calls out to explore the deep. People who've traveled there report profound freedom that comes from self-acceptance, find deeper satisfaction in their choices and feel confident forging their own path. Every journey starts with a single step and a decision to keep at it. But after you make the decision you're also going to need to know which steps to take.

Four Uncommon Sense Steps to Learning About Yourself:

1. Constantly assume there's more to you than meets the eye
2. Identify and sit with the right questions
3. Get feedback from the right people
4. Spend time with the right guide

The single most important thing adults who work with kids can do to help them grow into self-awareness is provide opportunities to reflect on their inner and external worlds. We can prompt them to explore what's going on inside and how external variables influence them- and vice versa. We can give them a few moments to think, both independently and out loud.

We can also serve as a mirror to them, reflecting on what we see and observe about who they are and how they come across. Too often, we assume that students know how they come across. They don't. And if they are thinking about it, typically, their mirror is distorted by their insecurities or ego. When we realize that, we can step into our role as adults who guide them into more self-awareness, without a plan other than helping them become the best version of themselves.

Summary: accurate self-awareness is a foundation for health and wellbeing. It's the basis for quality relationships, career satisfaction, effective leadership, and almost any worthy endeavor you can imagine. The people who lack self-awareness are typically the ones we try to avoid at all costs. You know the type- you probably work with one (or live with one). They aren't aware of how they come across, they're reluctant to own their mistakes, and they try to project a character of themselves that's inauthentic. Self-awareness is available to every person, but it requires a commitment to pursue it. Can you imagine a well-lived life without it?

11 How do you continue to learn about yourself?
SKILLS FOR ONGOING SELF-DISCOVERY

Patterns of thought and behavior get developed pretty early in life. Changing them requires extraordinary intervention, awareness, and decisive behavior over time. It's not easy to change what you do.

Since I was little, I have made a conscious effort to be funny. I like making people laugh, and I've always wanted people to think highly of me. Being funny portrays your intelligence and helps build quick connections with people. However, the style of humor I developed always leaned towards sarcasm and critique. Why? Because it's funny!

As a young adult, I met someone who became a mentor in my life. She was wise, kind, brave, and wanted to develop me into a leader, especially someone who cared for the poor and oppressed. One day she approached me with a question, wrapped in a compliment. She said how much she enjoyed spending time with me, especially since I brought life and laughter to conversations through humor. But then she asked me a question that changed my life. She said, "Have you ever considered how you might be funny without making people feel bad?" Ouch. I made a quick joke and got out of the conversation, but I didn't stop thinking about what she said. The thought, honestly, had never occurred to me, and it took me years of an intentional effort to find a sense of humor that didn't leave hurt feelings in the wake. That experience also taught me that there might be aspects of my life, personality, and interaction with others that I'm not aware of. Parts of me that I would want to change if I could get clear about them.

Dr. Dan Siegel is a clinical professor of psychology at UCLA and author of many books on parenting, mindfulness, and neural integration. He speaks directly to the critical function self-reflection plays for the developing brain in a TEDx talk for Education:

> "This part of the brain [the prefrontal cortex] allows you to be regulating your impulses. Does that sound familiar, controlling your impulses? It allows you to do that. It allows you to be aware of your feelings. It allows you to be aware of other people's feelings, and understand them. It allows you actually to be moral think about what's good for everyone, including the planet. It allows you to have intuition. It allows you to know where you've been in the past, where you are right now, where you go in the future, and it allows you to tune in on other people. That you get by reflecting on the inner world, mentioning and managing your feelings. It allows you to develop it when you have relationships that are supportive, like with teachers and with parents. And it allows you to develop all this so you're resilient."

Try reading that excerpt again, this time looking for the benefit of reflection that you wouldn't want your own children to have. Control impulses? Be self-aware? Have empathy? Be intuitive? Find clarity on the trajectory of your life? Demonstrate virtue? By guiding students to frequent reflection we can give them the capacity to both learn better AND become better humans.

Guided reflection can help students learn better in each subject area, too. Reflection helps students become more present, engaged, and motivated to learn. But the real purpose of guided self-reflection is to allow students to construct meaningful lives for themselves. Students are already subconsciously creating stories for themselves. Dan McAdams, father of the theory of narrative identity, says,

> "The formulation of a narrative identity is the central psychosocial challenge of emerging adults in modern societies. Equipped now with the cognitive software to construct causally and thematically coherent narratives of the self, and motivated to do so by cultural demands, ranging from parental pressure to economic necessity, that proclaim the time to 'get a life' is now, young men and women begin to put their lives together into full life stories that make sense of the reconstructed past and position them to move forward with purpose into an unknown future."

More than a few people in education say this isn't the job or purpose of school- these are the kinds of conversations that ought to be happening at home. I couldn't agree more that these kinds of discussions should be happening at home- but they often aren't. Not just because many families struggle to demonstrate wholehearted living, but also from an identity development standpoint, teenagers pull away from their primary caregivers as a survival mechanism to prepare themselves for life on their own two feet. Parents' opportunity to influence how their kids live their lives and make sense of the world significantly declines through these years.

The biggest and most prominent argument for why this kind of reflection should be happening at school is that it's directly tied to academic achievement. Students who have the opportunity to reflect on their lives, their values, their stories, and their goals and dreams become more engaged learners. Test scores increase. Graduation rates and college acceptance rates increase. That alone ought to get the attention of every teacher and school leader.

I'm not suggesting weeks or months or entire classes should be dedicated to guided self-reflection. However, that wouldn't be a bad thing- I'm suggesting that each teacher develop the skills and carve 2–5 minutes into each instructional hour to guide students to productive reflection in both peer and individual settings.

Suppose you agree with our two fundamental beliefs- that every student has the potential to be successful, and every student deserves the opportunity to construct a meaningful life for themselves. In that case, guided reflection is THE key.

Someone wise once said, *"The unexamined life is not worth living."* Now, that might be overstating things a bit, but the point remains: going through the motions of life on autopilot is far from real living. Just getting through the day is missing out on so much.

Underneath the surface are answers to critical questions so you can figure out what to do with your life. Unfortunately, there's no class in school to teach us how to understand ourselves. Rarely do we get the chance to learn that at home, either. But without a habit of self-reflection, we'll miss out on making the right decisions for the right reasons. We'll miss out on the opportunity to live an authentic life.

We've been helping military special forces transition to the civilian world for the past eight years. The gap we fill is somewhere between what a typical transition program would give them: networking skills, how to write a resume, using LinkedIn, etc., and what they need. Many have told us that when they enlisted as a teenager, the big questions about life were resolved for them in specific ways. They were given a significant role, a clear identity, an essential purpose, and a community of people to belong to. But, upon transition, the answers to those big questions no longer worked. They need to wrestle with the same questions they got to avoid years before.

Those questions are ever-present. The answers aren't fixed. The variables of life give shades of color and texture every day- if we're paying attention.

Many parents and teachers do right to teach kids important life skills. There are even programs designed to instruct those skills- like changing a car tire, opening a bank account, dressing professionally, and learning how to lease an apartment. But they miss out on the most important life skill: active self-reflection that leads to wisdom and engagement with life.

You can't teach it in a seminar or a lecture. It's not something you learn from a worksheet or a test. It's a skill that you pick up over time. You learn it by watching others engage in it- adults and peers. You develop the habit by practice and repetition.

If you have kids in your life, what are you doing to deliberately teach them the skill and the importance of ongoing self-reflection?

It starts with you. What's most effective for you to be thoughtful about your inner life: writing down your thoughts, doodling, talking out loud, or hearing someone else talk about their life?

- *What might keep you from being self-reflective?*
- *What could you gain if you developed a habit of self-reflection?*
- *What's an important question you have about yourself right now?*
- *How will you share your inner thoughts with the kids in your life?*

Summary: A key foundational element for being prepared to build a meaningful life is a habit of self-reflection. Self-awareness is a work-in-progress, not a one-time thing after taking a personality assessment. Each day brings a new opportunity to learn and grow, and without building a habit of self-reflection, we can miss critical insights. We can inadvertently carry on the residue of unresolved frustration, disappointment, or rejection into the next day- which doesn't do well for our mental health or social interactions. Can you imagine someone who's constantly unaware of what's going on underneath the surface of their life?

12 What do you appreciate about yourself?
INNER ACCEPTANCE

I can still remember the very first day of Middle School, hopping on the bus with all of my friends (or so I thought), everyone with their fresh kicks and new backpacks, ready and anxious to find our lockers and figure out what "dressing out" in P.E. really meant. Two things stick out about that day. A kid that I had gone to Elementary School with had grown nearly a foot and was super mean to everyone- all of a sudden. Another kid I had known for years as a friend and baseball teammate looked right at me, recognized me, and then turned away without saying "hi." Nothing felt the same, I was highly anxious every day, and I constantly felt in danger.

Something happens to the adolescent brain during the Middle School years. The brain suddenly wakes up to abstract thinking, and self-consciousness enters the picture. They become acutely aware that they're different; it feels like everyone is looking at them, and they start to judge themselves by their perception of how others react to them. The love and affection their parents gave them no longer matter; what matters is their peers and what they say, think, and do. They will settle with blending in so as not to be noticed or made fun of (is there any worse feeling than being humiliated?) and hope for acceptance into a group of friends.

This isn't just Middle School kids we're talking about, though; it's human nature! Have you ever met an adult who seems stuck in teenage comparison and insecurity?

When you're trying to find inner peace with external solutions like the number of followers you have, your athletic ability, your grades or test scores, or your number of likes on an Instagram post, you'll feel insecure, in danger, and constantly lacking. You won't think clearly, you'll easily neglect your values and virtues, and you will allow a destructive story about who's on top to become your controlling narrative.

Okay, that's a heavy concept.

The other way to say it is this: you're trying to drive your life towards specific outcomes so you can find peace and happiness, rather than allowing yourself to be drawn into the life that's meant for you. You might feel anxious, you might feel numb, or you might feel like a fraud.

What kids won't feel is confidence or contentment.

There are three fundamental messages everyone needs to learn to find security in themselves and their own identity:

You are not what you do.

You are not what you have.

You are not what others say or think about you.

Those are deep, profound life lessons that can only come through experience and reflection, and affirmation from others. When you can find inner acceptance in who you are and how you're uniquely wired, your life will come alive. You'll feel free to embrace your strengths and your weaknesses. You'll feel permission to pursue your interests and preferences, and you'll have the confidence to be your unique, quirky self.

That's the type of stuff we all want. It's mainly the type of stuff our kids need in order to make the transition well into healthy adulthood.

So how can we help our kids on the journey to inner acceptance? Two simple ways.

1. Find inner acceptance for ourselves and model it to them.
2. Guide them to become self-aware by reflecting on who they are, their unique makeup, and allowing them to share that out loud with peers

Here's a quick exercise you can facilitate, whether in your home or in your classroom- no matter the age of students you have. Ask them as a warmup exercise at the beginning of class (or dinner table conversation) to write down five things they appreciate or like about themselves and then share the top two or three out loud. This isn't a fluffy, self-esteem exercise from Saturday Night Live, these are seeds of opportunity for them to embrace themselves, be affirmed by others, and recognize the beauty of their own unique identity.

It's still a struggle for me, as I'm sure it is for you. To value me for who I am, rather than what people think about me or what I earn or have. I'm always going to be tempted to think I'm not good enough- there's evidence everywhere, from Instagram to bank accounts to parking lots to my own teenage kids who tell me so. Finding inner acceptance isn't something you do once at a therapy appointment or on a meditation retreat. It's a continuous practice and deliberate intention to embrace yourself in all parts, both the positive and the negative.

Pursuing inner acceptance is a gift we can give to the kids in our lives. We can model what it looks like, sounds like, and feels like to walk in freedom and grace.

Summary: A key foundational element for building a meaningful life is finding inner acceptance. The thing is, no one can do this work for you. Experiencing grace and compassion from people you trust will go a long way, but ultimately, the work is yours. Can you imagine a life well-lived without experiencing inner acceptance, instead of chasing validation and peace in external pursuits or from the approval of others?

13 What are you thankful for?
A HABIT OF GRATITUDE

I'll admit, I took most everything for granted when I was growing up. Yes, I did write thank you notes to my grandparents and brought teacher appreciation gifts to school that my mom bought. Generally, though, thankfulness was more about having good manners than an internal quality. Most things came easy to me, and my parents gave me a lot- resources, experiences, and love. It wasn't until much later, well into my adult years, that I began to both practice gratitude as well as feeling grateful.

A lot of kids are like me. They take things for granted. They don't have a broader perspective of who sacrificed for them or really have to work for what they get- nor should they. They're kids. But can you imagine a full-grown, mature, healthy adult who still takes life for granted? I can't.

Wise and emotionally healthy people would say: Everything is a gift. Everything. How do you learn that? How do you teach that?

Gratitude is something that you develop over time. You have to be guided into it. It has to be caught, not taught deliberately or overtly. You have to pause and reflect on what you've received. It's one thing to go through the motions of gratitude; it's another to express it to someone else. And it's an even higher level to feel it in an authentic way on the inside.

Okay, so how do you teach and train kids to be grateful?

1. You have to model it
2. Create an expectation for it
3. Carve out consistent time to practice it
4. Celebrate and rejoice every time you see it

It's easy to forget all the foundational elements a kid needs to transition to healthy adulthood. There's a lot to learn and a lot that's really important, like how to change a tire, how to interview for a job, and how to pay your insurance premiums on time. Those life skills can seem like the most important things we need to pass on. But what we're trying to do is provide clarity to parents and educators about the most important lessons.

It's so important, we build an entire curriculum about it (It's called Thanks to YOU).

It's hard to imagine someone who's always expecting to get what they want, when and how they want it. That would be an appropriate description of...a toddler, not a fully mature adult. Rather, feeling grateful and expressing it indicates a healthy, well-formed human. As much as our parents drill into us the notion of saying 'thank-you', or as many times as we write letters of thanks to our grandparents for a birthday card, becoming truly grateful on the inside is only something we can decide to do.

Just to warn you, expressing gratitude will cost you something. It can feel uncomfortable to admit that you appreciate what someone else did for you. It can feel vulnerable. You might even feel like you owe the other person something just by acknowledging your gratitude.

On top of that, no one can actually force you to be thankful. No one can convince you that it's worth it. It's something you have to test for yourself. You have to allow it to be something that doesn't just move your lips, but moves your heart.

- If you had to evaluate yourself on gratitude, what would you say? Is it a natural habit for you, or is it something you don't do automatically?
- Who's someone you know who readily expresses true, heartfelt gratitude? What do you admire about them?
- What's something in your life right now that you feel grateful for? How could you better express that gratitude?
- What kind of commitment would it take for you to make gratitude normal in your life?

The good news is, gratitude feels good. It releases hormones that make you literally feel better. It also helps strengthen your relationships with others. People like it when you acknowledge what they've done. It's great for your overall mental health, too. Not to mention, practicing gratitude requires you to be reflective, which will enable you to see patterns in your life and make wiser decisions overall.

Summary: A key foundational element for building a meaningful life is developing a practice of thankfulness and gratitude. Learning to receive life as a gift is a rare quality in the world. When you find someone who does, you'll find a person who's filled with life and light, freely able to share compassion and mercy and kindness wherever they go. The opposite type of person is, well, difficult to be around. It's hard to imagine someone living well who lacks an authentic appreciation for their lot in life.

14 What grounds you?
SKILLS OF SELF-MANAGEMENT

Is anyone feeling a little stressed out these days? Yeah- stress happens. It's a part of life. A healthy one, in fact. Psychologists are quick to remind us that stress is neutral, if not a positive experience. Stressful situations cause us to be stretched and grow.

The problem is when stress becomes a chronic situation.

Kids experience stress- a lot. Try to remember or imagine what a typical teenager goes through on any given day. Pressure from friends, from parents, from teachers, and from coaches. The constant threat of peer rejection. The feeling like you're always behind. The extraordinary pressure of impending college admissions. Siblings. Global pandemics.

Stress is actually a response we have to things called stressors. Stressors are situations, interactions, or events that trigger a threat response in us. Stressors can be external events happening towards us or around us, or they can be internal feelings. They can also be non-events (think about when your paycheck doesn't get deposited- that non-event has become a stressful situation!).

We all respond differently to stressors. For one person they feel threatened when they feel like someone doesn't like them. Another person might not bat an eye.

There are two dynamics that everyone can learn to manage stress effectively:

Diagnosis: the ability to understand how you've been triggered. To recognize what's happening to you on a biological and psychological level. To be able to identify the source of the stress.

Prescription: the ability to respond positively and productively to your own stress response.

In other words, we're talking about self-awareness and self-management, critical skills to being able to handle the complexities of life, especially through hard things.

We can teach kids to see and manage stress on two levels: biological and philosophical. On the biological side, there has been great research to help us understand what happens to us when we feel triggered by a stress response: in a split second the chemical epinephrine gets pumped into our brain, so our heart rate and blood pressure increases, muscles tense, and we start breathing quickly. Our entire biological system gets primed to GO- go fight, go run, or play dead. Key systems inside our bodies turn off, like critical thinking and reasoning, learning, creativity, and empathy.

When we're in a stress response, especially in chronic stress we can't:

- Think clearly
- Handle complexity
- Connect divergent ideas or viewpoints
- Recall our personal values or ambitions
- Connect with others
- Learn new concepts

Read through that list again, and consider what we go through and what our kids go through when we're in chronic stress. They can't learn or make wise choices until they work through their stress cycle. What if we learned to be more vigilant about our stress, and learned how to respond with simple, quick actions? What if we modeled and taught these things to kids?

From the book *Burnout: The Secret to Solving the Stress Cycle*, authors Emily and Amelia Nagoski share seven simple things we can do when stressed:

- Physical activity (30 min a day of exercise would be excellent, but even clenching every muscle in your body for a count of 10 will do wonders)
- Deep, concentrated breathing for a couple of minutes
- Have a positive social interaction with someone you enjoy
- Laughter
- Hug (for at least 20 seconds)
- A good cry
- Create something

Imagine if more teachers were equipped with this simple understanding as they designed their curriculum and lesson plans. Think about parents who learned to implement these simple tactics with their kids at home. Dream with us about kids learning this about themselves, and being guided consistently over time to pay attention to their stress response, taught simple strategies to manage it better, and praised when they took the initiative.

Stress happens, right? From a scientific perspective, anything that you perceive to be threatening is a stressor to you. That can come from multiple directions. It can be a threat to your autonomy, to your safety, or to your reputation. It can be a threat to your preferences, or a threat to a goal you're striving for. It doesn't matter where it comes from, what matters more is how you handle your reaction to it.

When we experience stress, the thoughtful, calm, and wise part of our brain shuts off. We can't think clearly, we can't be reflective about our values, and we can't make intelligent choices. That's a significant problem, and if we don't learn how to respond well to our stress, to work our way through it, we'll be worse off.

Sometimes, other people can help us manage our stress. Teachers can carve out time in class for a slow breathing exercise. Parents can help us see a broader perspective or get a snack. But as we get older, it's important to learn that we have to help ourselves. We have to learn how to manage our reactions to stressful situations. There's no way to control what happens, but we can learn more effective ways to respond.

So what will you do? Research says there are a few highly potent responses to working through a stress response. Regular exercise, deliberate breathing, connecting with friends, and laughter are all proven to help us move from overreacting to getting a clear head again. But, you'll need to find what works best for you.

- *What happens to you when you're feeling stressed out?*
- *What have you found to be the most helpful way to calm down when you're feeling stressed?*
- *What's something you know will probably help, too, but you haven't tried it yet?*
- *Who's someone you look up to that seems to handle stress really well? What do you admire about them?*

Summary: A key foundational element for building a meaningful life is developing skills for self-management. Since stress is unavoidable, we might as well find a way to manage it effectively. Typically, stress will lead us to spill out negative emotions onto others around us. Whether it's kicking the dog, speaking disrespectfully to cashiers, or being rude to your loved ones, it just doesn't go well. That's why it's critical to learn the skills of self-management. No one can do it for you; it's up to you. Can you imagine a life well-lived without it?

15 What's beautiful to you?
APPRECIATION OF BEAUTY

My mom got called in for a parent-teacher conference when I was in first grade. Typically, I was a good kid, but the teacher was concerned about my defiance during art lessons. I would never use the right colors to paint or color.

That's when they found out I was colorblind.

It hasn't been a huge issue in my life. Sure, I was crushed when I found out I couldn't become a Top Gun pilot. And, I have severe matching problems when it comes to picking outfits. But yes, in case you're worried: I CAN tell the difference between traffic lights. In fact, do you want to know the other top (read: ridiculous) questions people always ask me?

"Is it true you only see in black and white?" Nope- I'm not a dog.

"What color is this?" Hey- I'm not a circus sideshow!

Going to a Catholic high school with a uniform requirement was a major draw for me- I knew I would always match! (*"Is today a khaki shorts with a blue shirt day, or a blue shorts with a white shirt day?"*). Nowadays, I keep most of my wardrobe in the blues/greys/blacks- to avoid embarrassing my wife when I dress myself and go out in public.

I grew up always keenly aware that I was missing out on appreciating beauty like everyone else could. I think that's why I tried extra hard.

My mom, an artist herself, would often say something to remind me of my deficiency: "Do you see all the different colors in that sunset?" Or, "It's so sad you can't see how beautiful that painting really is..." She never said it to make me feel bad, but her comments served as a reminder to me that there was more beauty

BUT THEN IT ALL CHANGED

One morning in the summer of 2016, when I was getting ready for work, I overheard something on tv as my wife had The Today Show on in the background. They were talking about the latest scientific breakthrough: glasses that repaired colorblindness. Shocked- I ran to watch and started a Google search. There it was- with all of the relevant health issues in the world causing great harm to humanity, a company invested millions of dollars into research and product development to give a gift of color sight to the colorblind. And I had to have it!

I made a call- to my mom and made a plea: would she buy me the very expensive glasses? Notoriously generous, she quickly obliged and I made my purchase, only to be grimly disappointed with a 6-8 week backorder.

But, about a week later, I got a text message during the middle of the day from my wife: "Your glasses came today". Honestly, my heart skipped a beat. I canceled my afternoon meetings and raced home. All three of our kids were waiting at the door, thrilled to get me to try them on. But that's not where I wanted to see color for the first time. I had to go to a golf course.

A few minutes later we were all in the car, headed for my favorite course just a few minutes away. In the back of my mind, I kept thinking: "What if they don't work?" Or, "What if I'm not even color blind at all- just stupid?"

Then, pulling them out of the package, I put them on carefully. And everything changed.

The best way I've found to describe the first experience is to say this: Everything glowed. (For what it's worth, Gerard Manley Hopkins does a way better job in his poem, Pied Beauty).

I still have my colorblind glasses. A second pair, actually (I ruined the first pair). Honestly, I don't wear them every day. In fact, I try to save them for special occasions. I put them on when I'm having a day where I need to take a step back and reorient to what's real and what's beautiful. I wear them almost like a portal to meditation- they cause me to notice beauty in my wife's eyes, in the different colors of leaves in a tree, and in a sunset. Sometimes, I even put them on to go do the yard work- the weeds and dead spots on my lawn really pop.

But, more than anything, these glasses have taught me about building a meaningful life. The appreciation of beauty is a key part of the whole thing. Beauty is what makes life...beautiful. And beauty is all around us if we have eyes to see.

Summary: A key foundational element for building a meaningful life is making a regular practice of appreciating what's beautiful to you. What if we teach the appreciation of beauty as a life skill? Even asking the question: 'What's beautiful to you?' creates an expectation to look for it and places value on the pursuit of it. Can you imagine a life well-lived without beauty in it?

* In case you'd like to see the moment I first saw colors thanks to my color-blind glasses, we captured it on film: just go on YouTube and search my name and color blind. The video will pop up.

WRAPPING UP: IDENTITY

I want you to think back on the fifteen questions we just toured through on issues relating to a well-formed identity. Perhaps if you're honest, are there at least one or two of them you aren't so sure or certain about for your own life? It's relatively common for people to come up to me after speaking or presenting and jokingly say, "Is it too late for me to answer these questions?" It's not a joke, actually, whatever stage or season of life you're in is the perfect time to find clarity. But, do you know when it would've been even more helpful? When you were a teenager.

Consider all the important questions a teenager faces. Much more than just what they do for college or a job, those years form the foundation of who they will be for the rest of their lives. Imagine if you had just a few percentage points more clarity about your fundamental beliefs, core values, or inner acceptance? What would you have done differently if you truly understood your learning style or had skills of self-management?

What would've been different about the quality of your friendships if you had developed a habit of gratitude early on?

Now, I'd like to invite you to imagine what a life would feel like without clarity or confidence in yourself. Far from fulfilling, most people I talk to who are self-admittedly underdeveloped in their identity often describe an inner loneliness, anxiety, or lostness. They feel like their lives lack grounding or certainty, and everything seems disorganized from the inside out. A life without a clear identity is a life without faith in something bigger than yourself. It's unmoored; restless. That's no way to live, if you hold the vision of a meaningful life.

Next, we'll turn to questions of purpose.

SECTION TWO: CRITICAL QUESTIONS OF PURPOSE

One of my favorite holiday traditions is staying up late on Christmas Eve, after all the dishes have been cleaned from dinner and preparations have been made for the morning chaos, when our kids are asleep and the fireplace is lit. I finally get the chance to sit down by myself and watch the classic, It's a Wonderful Life. I know, it's old, saccharine, and overplayed. But I love the sentiment behind the story and the reflection watching it makes me consider as the year comes to a close. The question it always brings up for me is this: am I doing good at being here?

George Bailey is in many ways a simple character. A boy with big dreams to travel the world and make a big splash, he nonetheless gets stuck in his duty as the oldest son for his father's enfeebled savings and loan bank. While his younger brother goes off to college and adventures, his life is wrapped up in obligations and meeting expectations until at one point he snaps, feeling like the story of his life is so out of alignment with the vision he's always carried. Enter Clarence Odbody, the angel sent by God to help George find his way back to the life he's meant to live, a guide to discovering his true purpose.

George is a lot like all of us. We need help to see why our life matters. We want to know that what we do is worth it, that we make a difference. We want to feel alive and full of purpose.

The wake up call of the film is to avoid waiting for disaster to strike or despair to sit in before discovering your own reason for being. Traumatic, end-of-the-rope events and circumstances will certainly help you get there, but helping someone discover their purpose doesn't need to be so brutal. We can help students put together clarity for themselves about the reasons they exist, reasons for them to wake up every day, motivation to pursue growth and learning, and to harness the courage to make an impact in the world.

So every year I sit and watch the classic film. I think about my life, why I'm here, how aligned or misaligned I've been in the previous year to who I really am and pursuing what I think is most important. I reflect on the impact I've had on others, what would be different if I wasn't here or pursuing a life of purpose. It reminds me to be thankful, and it inspires me to continue down the bold path of a purposeful life.

16 What kind of person do you want to become?
A VISION FOR YOUR LIFE

Kids get asked all the time what they want to do when they grow up. High schoolers get asked what their plans are after graduation. College students get asked the same thing, with a big emphasis on work. But we never ask the most important question that foundationally will prepare a kid for success:

What kind of person do you want to become?

What a kid does professionally is important. We want them to be responsible for themselves and become self-sufficient. But it's only one part of the life equation- and it's not the most important. A key phrase we've used over the years that resonates with parents is, *"You can be successful in school and successful in your career but still fail in life."* We've found that if we put most of our focus only on what kids do for work someday, we miss the opportunity to help them build a meaningful life.

Too often we see people fall into the trap of only focusing on the externals of their lives, like a school to apply to, a job they're searching for, or a company they're looking to work for. Because what we do for work should express who we are, what our sense of purpose is, and what kind of contribution we want to make in our lives. When we guide students to reflect on their identity, purpose, ambitions, and vision for the kinds of people they turn into, the work part of their lives becomes a simpler problem to solve.

When we only focus on the externals, it's too easy to make decisions for the wrong reasons. A much healthier process is to postpone the externals like a job hunt or college selection until you get clarity about that big, important question.

When students don't know who they want to become, they lack the clarity and the confidence to make important decisions when they need to make them. Not to mention how many people discover later in life that the path they're on and the people they've become doesn't suit them (hello: midlife crisis). The choices students make affect them for the rest of their lives and will reinforce the trajectory they're on. If students don't have clarity about their character, they will lack the frame of reference to make wise choices or the courage to take risks or to build habits consistent with their ambitions.

We **can** help students find clarity about the vision they have for themselves in two distinct, surprisingly simple ways:

1. **Provide many examples of adults who embody healthy qualities.** That comes in the actual adults who work directly with kids, intentionally sharing who they are and what their personal lives are like. It involves those adults sharing vulnerable things about themselves and to express what motivates them and how their values drive their behavior. We can also offer examples

through the curriculum itself, especially characters in literature (English class) and historical figures (Social Studies/History). Students will determine what resonates with them by seeing values and qualities lived out in real life.

2. **Guide students to reflect and define who they want to be in each area of their lives.** We have plenty of opportunity and time to guide students to reflect in writing and verbal communication about who they are and who they want to turn into. We can do that in English class through journal prompts, we can do that through good Advisory or Homeroom curriculum, we can do that through assemblies and retreats, we can create mentoring programs, we can create Senior projects- we can do it. We just have to value it, prioritize it, and expect it.

Who you turn into isn't just left to chance. It's not just your natural state that unfolds over time until you realize you're done growing and have a result. Your future character is predicted by the clarity you have now and the many little choices you make now to live into the vision that you have. In The Moral Bucket List, author David Brooks calls those eulogy virtues in contrast to resume virtues. Eulogy virtues are those qualities that you seek to embody and the things you'll be remembered for by others, as compared to resume virtues as the accomplishments you hope to achieve. He urges people to seek eulogy virtues first and foremost.

Imagine if every student had that opportunity. (Imagine if you had *had* that opportunity!) For me, I know there's no chance I would've gone to college to study Accounting if I had reflected on the person I wanted to be- especially if they challenged me to explain why. All the ingredients of my character were available during middle and high school- I just didn't get the opportunity to think about it productively and put it all together. I mindlessly moved forward on a plan and life that belonged to someone else. But thankfully I had significant experiences and trained mentors who took me there in college.

Let's start expecting every kid to be able to answer this question before they graduate high school: *What kind of person do you want to become?*

Summary: A key foundational element for building a meaningful life is having a vision for your life. We get asked all the time about our professional goals, but rarely, if ever, does someone ask us about our goals for our character development. What matters more, at the end of the day- what we do, or who we are? There's no question that you will become someone. Your character and attributes will become predictable and knowable. The question is, will you like what you see?

17 What are your strengths?
OWNING YOUR STRENGTHS AND ASSETS

In college, someone asked me to give a brief announcement in a large group setting with about a hundred other students. It changed my life.

It wasn't the announcement, actually I can't even remember what it was about. The part that left a mark on me was right after when the adult advisor for the student organization came over and whispered in my ear, "You're great up front- you should speak more."

Before, I had never spoken publicly. I didn't even want to-it wasn't an aspiration of mine. But to hear that compliment and receive that affirmation- well, here I am, over twenty years later, and I make a living from being a public speaker.

It's kind of crazy when I think about it. One vote of confidence from an older guy I hardly knew at the time changed the entire trajectory of my life. He wasn't lying- I was good up front. It came naturally to me. But the crazy part is that I went to 15 years of school up until then without any other adult noticing that talent in me.

I wonder what would've happened if I had heard that when I was twelve.

I wonder what would've happened if I had never heard it.

One of my personal heroes, Ken Blanchard, wrote a book with Garry Ridge, the CEO of WD-40, called, Helping People Win at Work: A Business Philosophy Called "Don't Mark My Paper, Help Me Get an A". The book is a manifesto against the typical philosophy teachers, coaches, and managers take with their people. Most leaders, by default, assume wrongly that the best way to help someone else grow and develop is by criticizing them, calling out their faults and weaknesses, and providing negative feedback. Their theory, applied in practice throughout the WD-40 organization, asserts that the best way to help people grow and flourish is by focusing on their natural talents and strengths.

The Gallup Organization also endorses this theory with their Strengths Finder platform.

Students don't get taught through this lens, though, unfortunately. They still get taught that you have to be well-rounded, get an A in every subject if you want to have a successful future, and you have to get intervention support if you struggle in a particular subject. Students feel a ton of anxiety from their parents, teachers, and coaches when they don't excel.

How's that going?

My son gets really into things. When he was little, it was Thomas the Train before it was Lego's. Then it was Star Wars. He knows every character of every movie, show, novel, and graphic series. For an entire year, he woke up early before school to watch MLB Quick Pitch every day. He knew more baseball stats than most professional scouts. Lately, it's been mountain biking. It's not an overstatement to say he knows everything about mountain bikes. Every part, how they fit and work together, and which parts are quality. Even though he's still only 14, he landed a gig at a local bike shop to put bikes together for the store for their customers. For every three bikes he builds, he gets $25 of in-store credit. He's built over 100 bikes in the past month.

On one side, it's kind of annoying when he decides to get into something. He becomes obsessive. And it's expensive. But through a strength lens, what an amazing natural thing he has going on. We have no idea where it will take him- will he become an engineer? A teacher? A researcher? We have no clue where his interests will align with his passions. But we certainly can see his talent- and it makes him come alive.

Employers don't want well-rounded employees. They aren't impressed anymore when they interview someone who was really good at school. They want people who are passionate and committed to bringing their talents and unique perspective to solve problems at work. They want learners, listeners, and emotionally intelligent employees- not people who just meet expectations.

We have to learn to come alongside every kid and teach them to identify, own, and develop their natural talents until they become strengths. It requires a different mindset and a different practice. We, adults, have to be taught to look for talents and affirm kids in their natural wiring. We have to be curious and inquisitive about what goes on underneath the surface for each kid. We have to expand our understanding of what strengths are, knowing they can be academic strengths, people strengths, problem-solving strengths, creativity strengths, and more.

We have to find ways to validate the kids whose strengths don't match the performance management system of grading and test scores. We have to truly believe there's a genius in every kid.

We have to create continuous opportunities for students at every level to reflect on what makes them come alive and how they're uniquely wired, and encourage them to pursue their curiosity and interests.

But it all starts with pointing out the obvious. It starts with each of us whispering in a kid's ear, "You're really good at that- you should do it more."

So, how will you point out strengths in the lives of the kids around you?

Summary: A key foundational element for building a meaningful life is knowing and owning your strengths and assets. You'll likely get help along the way to understanding them- maybe by taking strength assessments or reviewing your report card or job performance reviews. Really owning and developing and building upon your natural talents, however, is something only you can do. You don't have to; most people don't. They do what's expected of them, or try to be someone they're not. But the truly content people are the ones who live in and out of their sweet spot. Can you imagine a life well-lived without it?

18 What are you going to do next?
A PLAN FOR THE FUTURE

When I was a kid in elementary school I consistently, year after year, had to be talked to about a behavior problem. I'd see it on my report cards and my parents would hear it in parent-teacher conferences:

"Scott's a good kid and a good student, but he's too easily distracted."
"Scott spends too much time daydreaming."

It was true- I had no excuse or rebuttal. Totally busted. I spent most of my class time somewhere else, dreaming about being the hero to my Little League team, winning the girl, or leading troops in battle. My daydreams were consuming, complex, and a lot more interesting than what was happening in school.

But somewhere along the path towards adulthood, I stopped daydreaming. I don't remember when it was, maybe Middle School when all of a sudden I had a lot more kids around, a lot more social pressure, and a bigger academic load. Or maybe it was High School when the pressure of getting prepared for college overwhelmed the free space in my mind. I don't remember when, but I know that I stopped.

I stopped dreaming about where my life was headed. I stopped fantasizing about what I could do, or who I could become. I put my head down and focused on the task at hand. For some reason, the older I got, the more disconnected I became from my imagination and creativity.

I know I'm not alone. Sir Ken Robinson has talked and written much about the lack of creativity and imagination in older aged school children. Creativity, imagination, daydreaming, and play are accepted and encouraged in little kids, but squeezed out of us the older we get.

But dreams are powerful. They shape our lives- the choices we make and the values we keep. Dreams can inspire the grittiest resilience or the toughest endurance. When we dream we have the power to be awakened to new possibilities, to overcome the biggest obstacles, and step into new realities that didn't exist before.

One problem I see, though, is that many people have ridiculous dreams for their lives. As we work with students in diverse contexts, it's unfortunately too common to hear students articulate plans and dreams for their lives that are tremendously farfetched.

You know what I'm talking about- the kid who is barely five feet tall and mildly uncoordinated who brags about playing in the NBA someday. Or the student who declares she's going to be a doctor, even though she's struggling to pull C's in her science classes and gets nauseous at the sight of blood. Or the students who vaguely talk about being rich someday, yet show very little grit or work ethic now.

It's a really awkward situation to be in. You WANT to encourage them, you WANT to support them, and you really want to see them be successful. But....come on!

Through YouSchool we want students to dream. We want them to have a compelling, inspiring vision of their future lives, where they could go, what they could do. We want them to see today as a step towards that future, and to be so clearly motivated to see their dreams come true that it changes their habits and principles.

In order for students to come alive today, they have to dream for tomorrow. But, they have to dream SOBERLY. We have to walk students through a process to discover who they really are, what they're actually capable of, and get clear about what's truly possible if they pour their heart and soul into a life plan. A realistic, sober dream will do more for them than a vague sense of who they want to be when they grow up. A sober dream will resonate with other people when they share it, enlisting real people to get behind them and support where they're headed.

A sober dream isn't a wish or a fantasy. It's an articulate vision of a possible future that inspires you and compels you to move forward that manifests itself through a lucid, attainable plan.

Summary: A key foundational element for building a meaningful life is having an articulate, logical plan for your future. Life is filled with uncertainties- job markets, health problems, relationship fallouts, and weather patterns. We can't control what events will unfold, but we can certainly participate in creating a future that aligns with who we are and who we want to be. Leaving everything to chance is one way to go, but rarely does that lead someone to the life they want to live. Rather, we have permission to thoughtfully plan for the future, taking deliberate steps to achieve our goals and dreams, and calibrate as we go.

19 What value do you bring to the world?
AN EXPERIENCE OF SUCCESS AT AN ADULT LEVEL

Recently, I had a humiliating moment when I was building shelves in our master closet. I'm no carpenter by any means, but I'm good at finding YouTube videos and giving things a try. My 14-year old son and I struck a deal- if he helped me with the shelves for a few hours, I would take him surfing early the following day. A couple of hours into the project, I got stuck trying to figure out how to secure a panel board to a ledger piece (long story). My son, in a very polite tone (with a hint like he was talking clearly and slowly as to an elderly person), calmly said, "Dad, if you just turn it around, it will fit perfectly."

Voilà. He was right.

Over the past few days, I've realized something about him- he's actually really good at fixing things. Like better than I am good.

I'm not sure why I was surprised by that- he's been fixing things since he was a toddler. Breaking toys and then rebuilding them. Buying parts for his mountain bike and drilling holes in aluminum to run brake lines through. He even has a job now at a bike store- for every three bikes he builds for them, they give him store credit to buy new parts.

I almost missed that about him. Being the modern dad that I am, I just sent him a text message that read, "Dude- I just realized, you're really good at fixing things! Like with the shelves, I would never have figured out how to solve that problem. And with bikes- you can take them apart and rebuild them. I'm not sure I know any adult who can do that as well as you!"

Then, it occurred to me. Our daughter has adult skills, too. At twelve years old, she's become really skilled at resolving conflict with her friends. We've noticed her doing that for years now. When she has a disagreement or there are hurt feelings, she empathizes, names her emotions, owns her part when appropriate, apologizes and forgives her friends. It's pretty remarkable!

Everyone yearns to add value. It's a core longing we all share. Knowing that what we do and are capable of doing has real value to another human.

Parents and educators, we have an opportunity. To take notice and be a mirror to our kids. To acknowledge and affirm the value they bring, especially when they're able to do something at an adult level. Just by noticing, affirming, and complementing we can not only make them feel seen and loved but also help steer them down a path that resonates with their unique design.

You might want to pay attention to how your kid:

- *Solves problems*
- *Engages in building new relationships*
- *Creates things with their hands*
- *Communicates an idea*
- *Uses technical know-how to resolve issues*
- *Shares their knowledge with others patiently and clearly*

My son will probably become a really skilled fixer- perhaps a mechanic or an engineer. My daughter will act as a peacemaker. Infinitely more likely if we continue to notice, affirm, and encourage them to express those parts of themselves.

Also, we can intentionally create opportunities for our kids to step up to the plate to be successful at an adult level. I love how Sage Creek High School in Carlsbad guides each graduating senior to give a TED-talk style presentation to share about a passion or service project they created- especially how they invite adults from the community to listen to their presentations and provide thoughtful feedback. The students are impressive, and they get to experience what it feels like to know their ideas and contributions have value to their community. That's a school project. Pretty cool, huh?

I love how the Culinary Arts program at Vista High School has students create dishes and a dining experience for the staff and admin every quarter. They give a fine dining experience to demonstrate their learning outcomes, and there's a pipeline of talented students who enter into the restaurant business year after year.

We all want to know that we have something valuable to bring, something meaningful to contribute. But we might miss out on that important lesson if all we do is encourage students to get good grades and get into a good college.

Summary: A key foundational element for building a meaningful life is having an experience of success at an adult level. It's these experiences that build our confidence and self-worth, which become signposts to help us navigate through the complexities of life. We can't ensure success, but we can take the necessary steps to take the risks. Can you imagine a life well-lived without finding something significant to contribute? (Hat tip to Brad Lichtman for the term: "Experience of success at an adult level")

20 What problems do you want to solve?
PROBLEM-SOLVING ORIENTATION

A few years ago my friend invited me to an NFL game to sit with him in the nosebleed section of a really boring Thursday night blowout between the Chargers and 49'ers. Halfway through the third quarter, I sensed some commotion behind and up above our seats where two guys were squaring off in a very junior high-looking smack-talk-throwdown. I'm sure a couple of 'your mama' insults were thrown, but I couldn't hear clearly since they were fifteen rows or so above our seats. I have to admit, there was a small part of my teenage psyche that hoped there would be a fight so at least we'd have some sort of excitement for the next quarter or two.

Three minutes went by and the guys were still standing nose to nose with merely taunts and expletives and unfortunately no fisticuffs- until a third guy came out of nowhere and sucker-punched one of the guys in the side of the head.

Queue: melee.

They grappled and locked horns and before I knew it started to tumble down the rows as they wrestled and each tried to get the upper hand. If you could picture the scene, the rows previously full of people between us and them parted like the Red Sea and the two guys rolled row after row until they finally landed…in my lap! Seriously, I was stuck between people on either side of me and had nowhere to go so I became the canvas to their showdown. Punches were thrown, curse words tossed, spit, and blood everywhere.

The security personnel finally showed up and pulled the guys off of me, but didn't seem interested in taking down my statement or checking my blood pressure. Adrenaline was flowing, and I thanked my friend for the best football game I'd ever been to.

Days later I found myself still thinking about the fight that I was a party to. I brought the story up in several conversations and noticed a strange sense of pride that I felt whenever I told the story. All that I really did was sit there motionless while two guys fighting each other on top of me. But still, I was in a fight!

There's something about being in a fight that makes everything come alive.

Now, I wasn't actually in a fight, just really close to one. But I've been reflecting on the idea of a fight for a while now, and come to realize that there's something about being in a fight (or you might say choosing to solve a problem or chasing a mission), that can both profoundly organize your life and also bring meaning.

Here are a few reasons why every kid should pick a fight with their life:

- There are a lot of fights to be had in the world. There is no shortage of meaningful problems to solve.
- You're here on earth to contribute and serve others.
- You have strengths, talents, and experience that can contribute to solving significant problems.
- You will come more alive and your life will feel more meaningful.
- You'll probably find other like-minded people and build quality relationships.
- The direction of your life will become more apparent and complex decisions will become simpler.

If you're not sure which fight to pick or which problem to solve don't worry about it or spend a lot of time deliberating. Just figure out what a sucker punch could be. Sign up to volunteer for a project or organization. Announce it to all of your social media friends. Buy a book to learn more. Invite someone to coffee to learn more about what they do. Sign up for the newsletter. Enroll in a class. Give money. Watch the documentary. Shout some expletives.

Whatever you decide to fight, make sure you fight something or someone. It could change everything.

But, forget trying to nail down the perfectly worded purpose statement for your life. Life is short, and you're here to get to work and solve problems. Instead, pick the next mission for your life.

For some people, their next mission is clear and obvious: Dominate the college admissions process. Graduate on time. Find a steady job. Become an effective manager. Move out of your parent's house.

For others, their next mission is more ambiguous. They aren't in any significant life transition, there are no immediate changes to their status, and the big-ticket items like work, friends, and where they live are stable. In that case, don't wait for a mission to grab you or be painted across the sky.

If your aren't sure what your next mission could be, here are a few categories to help you reflect, plus some personal examples to illustrate each idea:

- **Something that matters to you.** I really believe it's important for people to discover their unique talents and strengths. It was incredibly meaningful for me in college to have a mentor come alongside me and help me identify who I am at my best, and I've found that most people need someone else to help them understand themselves. It matters to me that the people I come in contact with find an opportunity through my words and actions to feel affirmed and grow in their own self-awareness about who they are at their best. My mission in life is to help unlock the potential in others by giving them the tools to understand themselves and unleash a great story in their lives. What matters to you?

- **Something you believe in.** I believe that youth sports are meant for kids to grow in confidence and character, learn about teamwork and resilience, and mostly, to have fun. I've noticed that many adults have forgotten that context and have ruined the spirit of sportsmanship and fun and replaced them with hyper-competition and drive for winning. I believe someone needs to help refresh people's minds about the purpose behind youth sports, and invite other parents to return to a wholesome spirit. What do you believe about how the world ought to be?

- **Something that is noble.** Do you know what's noble, in my opinion? Providing for your family. Choosing a more manageable load at work so you have more time and energy to invest in your kids when you get home. Deciding to be a stay-at-home mom for a few years. Giving your kids a stable home life and access to resources and opportunities that you didn't have when you were growing up. Those kinds of choices would be looked down upon to some ambitious people. But you might find that your work is a means to another end, a far more important end. What do you consider noble?

- **Something that you think would be right.** I have always had an affinity for old people. I like the way they talk about the 'old days', the way they wink at you and get away with it, and say inappropriate jokes. Since I'm raising my kids in a town that was initiatlly designed as a master-planned retirement community, there's no shortage of old folks driving on the wrong side of the road near our house. The few times I've gone to a retirement home to visit some elderly people, I've heard a consistent theme: their gratitude for you spending a few minutes with them because rarely do they receive visitors who are interested in their lives and stories. It doesn't sit well with me to think about old people who are rich with wisdom not to have the opportunity to be a gift to others through their time. I can imagine a mission where I invest my energies in creating a structure for people to visit the elderly near them. What comes to mind for you to fix something that just isn't right?

- **Something that brings justice.** If you're going to fight for something and you're not sure what to fight for, you probably couldn't go wrong by fighting injustice in your hometown. If you're paying attention, you'd have a hard time watching a local news segment without coming across a real injustice just a few minutes from your front door. What injustice have you noticed lately that keeps popping up in your point of view?

- **Something that creates beauty.** My mom has an uncanny ability to create beauty in the spaces around her. She can see with her eye when a picture is hung too high on a wall, and when a cheesy looking table at a garage sale could be repainted to perfection. As a serial home shopper, she's purchased and redesigned over a dozen homes, and each one she leaves her stamp of beauty on for the next homeowner. When people have been smart enough to ask, she's offered her talents to their homes and help them create beautiful spaces for their families. What could you do to create beauty for people in your life?

- **Something that brings order.** I have a friend named Blake who radically changed careers to go into Accounting and Finance so that he could lend his knack for providing order and structure to health care companies that make devices used in hospitals for cancer patients. He wants his company to run efficiently because he knows that the more aligned structures on the backend will provide more life-saving and life-preserving devices for hurting people. His mission might not be as dramatic as a surgeon's, but just as meaningful to him. What systems, organizations, or structures in your world could benefit by having more order and alignment?

- **Someone who is overlooked.** There are plenty of people who are overlooked. I have a friend named Sarah who moved with her husband and two kids to live in the inner city of San Diego to run a non-profit that develops youth to be leaders in their neighborhoods. She's dedicated her life to redirect resources and create sustainable structures for overlooked youth to be invested in. Who do you think is overlooked in your community?

If you don't have a passionate cause right now, that's ok- a lot of people don't. It could be that picking a mission for the next 6 months to 6 years would not only organize your life but also galvanize your energies and efforts in a dramatic way. If you're feeling a little stuck or a little lost, then try putting pen to paper and reflecting on the questions offered above?

Summary: A key foundational element for building a meaningful life is having a problem to solve. A problem to solve will help you orient and organize your life and investments of time and energy. It will give you a compelling reason to wake up every day, and a drive to get better so you can provide more value. Can you imagine a deeply satisfying life without a problem to solve?

WRAPPING UP: PURPOSE

I want you to imagine someone who has all the confidence in their beliefs and values, who feels certain about their unique identity, has processed their past wounds and lives confidently in their own skin, and yet has no compelling reason to get up every morning. They can tell you with eloquence about their beliefs and worldview, but there's nothing that inspires them to act boldly and they have no real experience with what it means to bring significant value to someone else's life. There's no big problem they want to solve. They're uncertain about their own talents and strengths and

A life without purpose is a life without hope.

There's an old proverb that says "Hope deferred makes the heart sick, but a longing fulfilled is a tree of life." When you don't have someone counting on you, or a team who needs what you bring to the table, or a social problem that will not get solved without you, it can make you sick. People need to be needed, not just feel obligated.

And, unlike George Bailey's experience in *It's a Wonderful Life*, we don't want kids to have to wait for someone to swoop in and show them why we're here and remind us what value they bring to the world in thirty years. We can help them figure it out now, and give them the tools they'll need to continuously reflect on their purpose.

SECTION THREE: CRITICAL QUESTIONS OF BELONGING

The primary quest for a teenager is about acceptance and belonging (Really, it's for any age). That's what drives them. Have you ever been around a teenager as they get dressed in the morning for school? What happens when you suggest that the sweatshirt in their closet would be "just fine"? Or, can you remember a time in your teenage years when you were left out of something- a party, an event, or maybe no one invited you to the dance? It's crushing.

For teens, the pursuit of acceptance and belonging triggers a survival response in them. They implicitly understand that the tribe they've belonged to in the past- the family who's fed them, protected them, and nurtured them, is going to kick them out of the cave soon. They have to find a new tribe, and fast. The problem is, how do you develop relationships that aren't just about fitting in and looking alike, but where you're accepted with the same level of commitment as a family? That's the tricky part.

In hindsight, most of us eventually shed the friendships we built during our teenage years. Sure, there might be a couple of people you stay in touch with and share a beer with when you're home for the holidays, or there might be one friend that you stick with throughout your life. But, for the most part, we move on to different people and start over when we reach our twenties. It's hard to make the transition to adulthood and reset other people's perceptions of you they developed when you were younger- especially when you were trying so hard during your teen years to act like someone you weren't.

Some people, however, never find their tribe. They have relationships and acquaintances, but there's no one who knows them at a deep, authentic level. There's no one who really knows them without their pretenses and defenses up, and there's no one they can truly lean on. That makes for an incredibly lonely existence.

Loneliness is at an all-time high and continues to rise in our country. Projecting that into the future: what's going to happen to the nature of relationships in twenty years, when so many teenagers are currently interacting with people in a completely virtual environment (whether it's for school, for social media, or for gaming)?

Isolation is a killer.

It's also the source of stunted growth. It's really hard to figure out who you really are and what really matters without people who will tell you the truth, and stick with you regardless of how you respond.

Authentic friendships aren't easy, or natural for most people. Kids need help learning how to build healthy relationships- we all do. It's the most important part of our lives, and yet there's no formal or effective informal education for it. There can be, though, and it starts with you, and it starts with figuring out what the right conversations are they need to have.

21 What do you do to put others first?
A SERVICE ORIENTATION

Here's an unsettling question: given who your kids are today, do you expect them to naturally and automatically put the interests of others ahead of their own when they're adults? Ouch, right?

A quick detour into our family lore:

"Mom, have you seen Tracey?"

"Well, we need to tell you something. You know that family down the street who just lost their dog? Your dad felt really sad for them and so this morning after you went to school he took Tracey down and gave her to them."

That's one of the many true stories my mom tells about the kind of dad my grandfather was to her when she was little. He was generous to a fault;

selfless even when it got him into hot water with his family. When he passed away he had very few possessions to divide or deal with- he had given most away over the years. Fud was his nickname, and if he had a problem it was in giving too much away. (My mom did get her dog back, by the way.)

I'm not sure how Fud became so generous. Certainly, he was a big feeler and had an extra dose of empathy. If you needed something and he had it- whether it was a tool, a piece of furniture, or the family dog- it was going to end up on your side of the fence shortly. Sometimes I wonder why I'm not more like Fud in that way.

I also wonder what it will take to teach my kids to be generous and convince them that the better way to live is to put the interests of others ahead of their own.

I know it's not just my problem, either, and the problem is not just about being generous with possessions. I'm more and more aware of times and spaces where I'm withholding what I have when what I have (strengths, energy, perspective, skills, etc) could actually solve a problem, add value, and bring something meaningful to others. I notice those situations at work- meetings I'm in or teams I serve on. I notice those moments in my neighborhood when I too quickly close the garage and go inside rather than engage with my neighbors. I've withheld what I have for my kid's sports teams, at church, with friends, and with my family. I'm not trying to paint a picture of my selfishness- I don't think anyone would describe me that way. Nor am I trying to suggest that we can be selfless and generous at all times- I'm a huge proponent of self-care and living within your limits.

What I'm suggesting is that we have a window of opportunity to show our kids the importance of serving others.

Who do you want your kids to become?

Fud embodied my vision for what a genuinely generous person thinks like, sounds like, and acts like. I reflect on him often and the example he set for me, but I'm not sure if I've truly, deep down decided that I want to become as generous as he was. If you have a vision for your kids becoming people who are selfless, sharing, and generous, then what would they say, how would they think, and what would they do differently?

There's a pearl of ancient wisdom that's grounded in centuries of depth: to those who have been given much, much is expected. In case you need it translated into contemporary language: If you've got something- put it to use. Give it away. Step up. Quit holding on or sitting back. Beyond just a wise saying, I've found this principle best realized through active reflection. Read the moment- what does this moment call for? What problem are we stuck on? What does my company or teammate or friend or neighbor need right now? Then do a self-inventory: what do I have at my disposal? Which talent, skill, strength, or past experience can I lean on and put to use? If you've got something, then doing even a few seconds of self-reflection can help you see reality clearly and choose to step up with what you have.

Sometimes you're called upon to step up to serve and take on a role you don't prefer. For instance, I get an email at the start of every soccer season from the league president that makes a clear, unashamed ask for parents to serve as volunteer coaches. Also, I've been tasked several times in the past by a boss to take on an administrative role for a project- the last thing I want to do. But I do it because I respect my boss and I have the capacity to help. Or, think about the neighbor who rings your doorbell, wondering if you have jumper cables. In most scenarios, though, at work, in your family, in the organizations you participate in, there aren't clear requests or even clear problems.

Likely, the situations are ones that you find yourself complaining about. For instance, when I'm not the coach for my kid's sports teams I can easily be a lawnchair critic, hanging out in the shade wondering aloud why the coach is running a disorganized practice. Or make quiet snide remarks to a co-worker when someone else runs an inefficient meeting. Subtly, without noticing, I can easily find myself feeling little to no responsibility to step up and contribute my talents and strengths- especially when I'm not asked. It's like I dismiss myself from taking ownership if someone in charge doesn't give me the explicit permission. The wiser I become, the more I'm realizing that I don't need to wait for someone to give me permission, I can offer what I have in a humble posture, roll up my sleeves and get to work.

How can we expect our kids to become people who instinctively serve others unless we deliberately teach them? It starts by us modeling that kind of life for them, and then asking them a really important question many, many times over the years: What did you do today to put others first?

Summary: A key foundational element for building a meaningful life is having an orientation to put others first- can you imagine a healthy adult, thriving in a family, workplace, or community who doesn't regularly or naturally put others first? Nope! In fact, putting others first has been a theme we've been trying to instill since preschool.

23 What's your story?
ABILITY TO TALK ABOUT YOURSELF

When people ask me what I do for a living, I realize that there are a few different ways to answer that question. I could tell them about my title, or my profession. I could tell them about the field or industry I'm in. I could tell them about what I used to do, what I do now, and what I'm hoping to do next. Or, I could tell them about what I actually do all day long- the nature of my work.

Me? If I described what I actually do for work, I'd say I have thoughtful conversations for a living. That's the summary. But what does it mean?

It's one thing to be able to tell your story in a clear way. It's another thing for your story to be helpful for someone else to know how to respond.

The most significant question your kids will be asked throughout their lives:

Who are you? What's your story?

It's the question that gets asked again and again throughout our lives: the first day of school, on first dates, in college essays, job interviews, loan applications, from new roommates, co-workers, supervisors, neighbors, and Starbucks baristas. Depending on who's asking, your answer probably gets filtered down a particular lane.

How do most people typically answer? With facts.

"I'm a sophomore."
"I'm from Orange County."
"I'm the intern."
"I'm a basketball player."

Most people respond by sharing their geography, titles, roles, organizations, or relationships. I get it; those facts provide some context. But, facts leave the person listening with the burden of making meaning out of those facts, and too often the story gets lost in interpretation.

If we don't learn how to tell our story effectively, we won't be fully equipped to construct and design a meaningful life. Everyone has to learn to express themselves and communicate who they are, where they come from, what's most important to them, what makes them unique, and where they're headed.

Telling your story is the prerequisite for building authentic relationships. If you don't know how to talk about yourself, share your story, express your ideas, and communicate who you are, people won't know what to do with you. They won't be able to really know you, and your relationships will remain shallow.

If this is the question that's going to get asked time and again in your life, and if it's the question that determines how people understand you, whether they want to date you, hire you, or be friends with you, don't you think you owe it to yourself (and to others) to do the hard work to have a really great answer?

There actually is a way for your kids to develop a thoughtful, real, relevant answer to who they are. Storytelling is a learnable skill that everyone can develop.

Here are a few guideposts to help you and your students start the process of becoming effective storytellers:

- **Act as a private investigator in your own life.** Make observations about how you come across to others (shy or reserved, loud and dominant, intense and focused, laid back and easy-going, etc). In other words, build a consistent habit of self-reflection.
- **Ask close, trusted Advisors how they describe you to others.** Avoid being defensive, instead, listen to their words and ask them to help you see what they see. Yep- ask for feedback.
- **Find accurate role models** or fictional examples that help you understand yourself better and explain yourself more clearly. Such as, I'm the Michael Jordan of the internal auditing world- I work harder than anyone else and take riskier shots.
- **Get a lot of reps.** Intentionally put yourself in situations where people will ask you that question, and try a new way to explain yourself each time, taking careful note of how people respond, their facial reactions, and the depth of conversation that follows

each version.

No one can really tell your kid the best way they should answer the question. It's up to them to figure it out, and up to them to decide how to tell their story. You can help by letting them practice, by being an accurate mirror to them over the years, and by putting them in situations where you know someone will ask them.

The next time someone asks your kid that question, will they be ready? How about you?

Summary: A key foundational element for building a meaningful life is the ability to tell your story in a clear, compelling, authentic way. It's important for building good friendships. It's key if you ever want to find a mate. It's really vital if you want to be a contributing employee or effective leader. No matter which way you slice it, learning to tell other people about who you are, where you come from, and where you're going is a fundamental part of doing life well.

24 Who are your people?
AUTHENTIC FRIENDSHIPS OF BELONGING

Countless studies have proven the value of having close friendships with our psychological and physical health. People who have close friendships do better academically, at work, economically, physically, psychologically, and spiritually. Being connected to friends means you're less likely to feel depressed or anxious, more willing to take risks, and you'll make more money throughout your lifetime. From a logical perspective, I doubt anyone would challenge the benefits of close friendships.

Then why do so few adults (adult men especially- sorry to pick on you!), have close, trusting friendships with at least a couple of people? Why is loneliness on the rise so dramatically? We can point to the ubiquity of smartphones and social media as sources of our disconnection, but blaming them can only get you so far.

One of the foundational questions we guide people to process in The YouSchool is about their friendships and the experience of belonging they have with others. We know the importance of meaningful friendships and have seen firsthand that even if someone can get clear about their purpose, career path, clarify their core beliefs, have a vision for a life of impact but they don't have close friends- then they still deeply long for more meaning in their lives. If we had to choose, we'd instead guide people to healthy, authentic friendships than to meaningful work.

In our work with thousands of adolescents through Middle and High Schools, we invite them to reflect on their understanding of friendship, their experiences with friends so far in their lives, to project and imagine the kinds of friendships they'd like to have in their lives, and then define what type of friend they commit to being to others. As a part of that process, we ask them to talk about how their parents have modeled friendship to them, and reflect on what they've learned from their parents as it relates to friendship. One thing we hear consistently, regardless of the demographics of the school, is kids talk about how they don't know if their dads have close friends at all. We hear that from inner-city kids, students at continuation high schools, and students in high-achieving schools and wealthy neighborhoods.

As a simple observation, although friendship is an innate desire found inside everyone, the art of practicing healthy friendship is a skill that can only be learned by watching it modeled by others. If you don't learn from your parents how to have healthy friendships as adults, you're going to struggle to figure that out, too.

I distinctly remember one of the most difficult, awkward conversations of my life. It was Christmas break during my second year in college, and I called an acquaintance of mine to ask him if he wanted to be better friends with me when we got back to school.

"Umm, hi- Dave? Uhh, yeah, this is Scott. I'm calling to tell you that I liked getting to know you this past fall and, um, I was wondering if you wanted to, like, be better friends when we get back to school."

Can you say A-W-K-W-A-R-D? I can't remember how Dave responded except it was a definitive yes, and a few years later we took turns standing next to each other as Best Man in each other's weddings.

Building friendships that matter to both sides sometimes happens naturally and organically. It seems like some people are born into a healthy network of quality people who support, encourage, and help them. Others have that extra special gift of being charismatic and attractive to people around them and great people flock in their direction throughout their lives. But those are tiny minorities of the population. There's no question that everyone wants and everyone needs multiple relationships of deep connection for their personal and professional lives to flourish, in order to experience deep meaning and connection in life. Most people will have to be intentional, strategic, and vulnerable if they want to build a healthy squad.

Here's our step-by-step guide for how to help your kid (or yourself) build their own healthy group of friends:

- **Have a clear vision**: the first and most important step is to take a step back to imagine what kind of friends you want and need in your life for you to thrive, and what kind of friend you want to be. You might think of a film you've seen or a book you've read where the vision you saw for deep friendships moved you in some way or the relationship someone had with a mentor inspired you. You might use a journal to write down the different kinds of people you'd love to have in your life (think: mentors, confidantes, role models, advocates, etc). We encourage you not to feel ashamed if you're in a place where you'd love to find more or different kinds of people in your life. Your longings and desires for friendship and support are good and noble.

- **Decide to go for it**: once you've clarified a clear vision for the kind of squad you long for, there's going to be a moment where you need to decide to go out and build it. Similar to the awkward phone call I made, I decided that the kinds of friends I hoped for weren't going to just drop in my lap, so I decided to take the step to identify someone I liked and respected and pursue a friendship with him. You probably won't have a mentor show up in your life unannounced. You likely won't stumble upon people who will advocate for you. You have to build your relationships intentionally.
- **Invite that new friend to an experience with you: a coffee, a meal, an event (make sure you pay!)**. Friendships can't be built without shared experiences and time together. Consider inviting them to activities that they'd most be interested in.
- **Serve them in some way**: send them a link to an article you think they'll find interesting or valuable, make an introduction to someone on their behalf, or consider giving them an endorsement on LinkedIn if that's appropriate. Friendships that are built on you serving first will go a long way.
- **Share your fries, your opinions in a respectful way, your connections, and your encouragement**.
- **Spend more time asking curious questions than you do talking about yourself**. Get to know who they are, what they like and don't like, and what their ambitions are. Ask for their opinion, for their advice, and for their recommendations.

- **Be open to their generosity towards you, to their advice, to their group of friends, and to their perspective.** You don't need to morph your life to resemble theirs or try to mirror everything about them, but if you're open to them then you'll continue to receive them as a gift.
- **Be generous with your time, the attention you pay towards them, with your compliments, and with picking up the check.** Surprise them with unexpected gifts, and go out of your way to make them feel unique and valued.
- **Last, but not least, be consistent in your direction towards them.** Be consistent in inviting, in serving, in sharing, and in asking. The more consistent you are towards them, the deeper the trust and bond will be.

There's nothing more important or meaningful than the people you travel through life with, so make sure you're building the best squad possible.

So what type of people does everyone need? Here are a few categories of friends everyone should be looking for:

- **Confidante**: a confidante is someone that you can trust to share everything with. They won't recoil in disgust or judgment. They aren't quick to offer advice or fixes. A confidante is likely your best friend, someone you can always count on.
- **Airport driver**: let's say you have a flight coming up at 5 am. Who do you call? Everyone needs someone they can count on in a pinch. The friend who offers to help you move. The person you expect to give you a present on your birthday.
- **Neighbors to take your trash can in**: our neighborhoods have changed context over the last two generations, but still, it's important to have relationships with the people you live around

whom you can count on to take your trash in, or pick up a package for you.

- **Monday Night Football buddy**: who do you invite over when you want to watch the big game? The person who is fun, they share interests with you and can be generous with good conversation. This is the person who doesn't complain when you don't call them for a couple of months, either.
- **Advisors**: in the YouSchool world, an advisor is someone you trust to listen to you, get to know you, and both encourage you and speak a hard truth to you. An advisor is someone who is full of wisdom, is a great listener, and can help you understand deeper things happening in your life. Often an advisor will be older than you but doesn't need to be.
- **Guide**: everyone needs direction in their lives, someone who has already walked down a similar path, has been through similar challenges, and has the empathy to understand what you're going through. A guide is someone who can come alongside you and invite you to take hard steps to grow.
- **Role Models**: you need people to look up to, people who are demonstrating what life looks like well lived, in a style and flavor that resonates with who you are. Your role models can be people that you know (ideal), or they can be public figures. They can be alive or dead, fictional or real, and not one person will fit into every category for you.
- **Advocates**: these are people who can sponsor you to others. They have access and power, and they have the ability to offer their credibility on your behalf. This might be a teacher who offers a college recommendation letter, a family friend who can get you an interview for an internship, or a boss who can champion your talents for a new opportunity.
- **Access to Resources**: okay, you might cringe a little at this one because this is basically the 'rich and powerful' part of your

squad. At some point in your life, you'll likely find a mission or a cause that will require more resources than you have at your disposal. Whether it's starting a company or raise money for a non-profit, having people who are in your circle who have access to significant resources will be key.

- **People to serve**: we'll deal with issues of morality and generosity elsewhere, but for this conversation, I'll say that it's vitally important for your mental, emotional and spiritual health for you to have direct contact with people to serve. Serving people gives you an opportunity to exercise your talents, it connects you with a deeper meaning; it reminds you of what's most important, and it teaches you about yourself and your ongoing growth to maturity.
- **Diversity**: as a final word about building your own squad, it's important to avoid creating your own echo chamber where the voices you hear and the perspectives you learn from have the same accent, metaphorically speaking. You need to have people in your close circle who come from different walks of life than you, have distinctly different perspectives than you, and who can shape you into an integrated person.

Summary: A key foundational element for building a meaningful life is having close, interdependent relationships with others. More than almost any other question or asset we've discussed, having people in your life you can count on, lean on, share with, and to serve is what makes our time on earth rich and significant.

25 What do you do to connect with others?
RELATIONSHIP SKILLS

"One is the loneliest number that you'll ever do" — Three Dog Night lyrics

There's one moment in my life that sticks out above the rest as the loneliest moment I've ever had. It was the end of my freshman year in college, and as I was packing up my dorm room to head back home for the summer I had a chilling thought: If I don't come back to school in the fall, no one would notice or care, nor would I miss anyone here. I had a notion that the first year in college would be more than fun and games- it would be the time of my life and ground zero for lifelong friendships. In a moment of honesty, I realized that despite the hundreds of other students I had met, no true bonding occurred and the residual feeling I drove home with was regret, sadness, and loneliness.

"Being deeply lonely seemed to cause as much stress as being punched by a stranger." — Johann Hari, Lost Connections

The experience of feeling lonely, where our desires for connection, bonding, and supportive friendships far exceed our reality, is described by many as the worst feeling in human nature. Studies in recent years have shown the adverse effects loneliness has on our mental and physical health. Recent trends in technology and smartphone ubiquity have served to increase our suffering from loneliness, and apparently, "it seems the younger you are, the lonelier you feel." No matter the cause, feeling lonely is an awful human experience.

Ancient philosophers, though, have been exploring loneliness for centuries and the idea that it's possible to transform loneliness into profound, transformational experiences of solitude and depth. They've taught us that loneliness can serve as an indicator of change and a threshold to seek out transformation and freedom.

So what can you do to examine your own experiences of loneliness in a productive way for you to grow closer both to internal peace and friendships that lead to your flourishing? Here are a few steps to consider:

- **Embrace your loneliness**: most people avoid uncomfortable feelings at all cost. With easy access to technology and other distractions, the silence of loneliness can easily become deafening, and if you're a human then it's likely that you have your own version of quick-fixes to quiet the noise. Maybe it's online shopping, responding to email, scrolling through a social media feed, binge-watching a Netflix show, texting ridiculous GIFs to your friends, or reading Trump's latest tweets. Whatever it is, if you're using that noise to distract you from the discomfort of loneliness, then your invitation is to stop what you're doing and feel what you're feeling. Yes, the feelings will become more intense. But the longer you avoid them, the more they will chase you. Maturity looks like welcoming those uncomfortable feelings and allow them to teach you what they need to teach you.

- **Share your lonely feelings**: the next time you're in a conversation, even small talk, with someone who matters to you and they ask you about how you're doing lately, then take a deep breath and then admit how you've been feeling lonely. Don't add much to it, or throw in qualifiers like, "But it's good", or jokes like, "I guess that's what you get for being so smart and attractive", but allow them to hear the pain that you're going through. They might not respond correctly, and this might not be the only time that you need to share your loneliness, but it's a healthy, positive step towards reaching out and connecting with someone on a deeper level.
- **Reorient to beauty**: when we feel lonely, it's the worst. Life seems small, you see things through a negative lens, and the world seems out to get you. Choose to reorient to what's good and beautiful around you. Perhaps that's as explicit as using a gratitude exercise, a nature walk, or turning on music that inspires you.

Your loneliness is a reminder to you that your soul is in need of connection. When you feel lonely, you need to know that you have choices to make, choices that help you reconnect and transform the painful, negative experiences of loneliness into peace and freedom.

When I grew up, I was pretty normal. Meaning: I played outside with friends all the time. These days, hardly anyone plays outside anymore. When my wife and I first had kids we learned about something called a playdate- a new concept invented by preschool moms.(In case you grew up in the 80's and don't have kids yet, let me explain. A playdate is an arranged marriage of sorts where typically two moms collude to get their kids together and manufacture a friendship.)

I remember one playdate I went on when I was a kid, although we didn't call it that. The mom of a kid from school called my mom to arrange an afternoon to play and my mom dropped me off at his house for an hour or two. I didn't really know him, we had never interacted at school, and that afternoon I remember feeling really stressed out because how intense he was, quick to anger he became, how controlling he was, and generally…not fun. I knew that was the last time I would ever 'play' with him again. But, the problem was, his mom really wanted to encourage us to be friends and mentioned many, many times how she thought I was a "good kid" and wanted to set up more playdates. Thankfully, my mom picked up on my radar, and in classic mom fashion, feigned interest with promises to "call her soon". That was the first (and only) playdate I had.

Lately, though, I've been re-thinking the idea of playdates and pondering how to reimagine them for teenagers. A lot of students have opened up to me over the years and shared that they feel lonely a lot, brought upon by packed schedules, fear of vulnerability, smartphones and social media, and cultural shifts.

We know that establishing deeper, more consistent bonds with a few people can change our lives and provide the meaning our souls long for, but it's not so simple, is it?

I believe that teenagers, young adults, and parents should reconsider the idea of a playdate and learn to be just as intentional as a young suburban mom. If you'd like to build better friendships, here's how you can repurpose the lost art of the playdate to develop your relationships:

- **Make a list**: who comes to mind as someone you're drawn to, someone you like, someone you respect, someone you admire, someone you'd like to become more like, or someone you'd like to spend more time with and get to know?

- **Think through what you want to do**: what do you enjoy doing? Mountain bike, go to the movies, try new restaurants, knit sweaters, play pickleball, or surf? Think through what you enjoy and invite them to join you.

- **Invite someone to join you** (and don't give up if it's hard): the best friendships begin by doing something, and you can't do something together unless you invite them. Don't worry if they don't enjoy the same thing- yet, just be bold enough to ask them to join you. If it's hard to find the time on your calendar- don't give up! Keep trying until it works out- or until they tell you to buzz off!

- **Be strategic about the time**: before you spend time together, spend a few minutes thinking through how you'd like your time together to go. What do you want to get to know more about in their lives? What topics of conversation could you bring up that would spark a good discussion? What would you like to share with them about your life or what you're thinking about? If you don't intend to take the conversation somewhere, you might miss the opportunity to take it somewhere significant. It wouldn't even be a bad idea to make a note in your phone about questions you'd like to ask or topics you'd like to bring up.

- **Ask again**: after you've spent time together if you enjoyed being with them and look forward to spending more time with them, then…ask them again!

- **Say 'yes' more often**: if you get invited to spend time with people who fall on your list above, then do what you can to move things around in your life and join them.

Friendships, especially close ones, don't just happen. After college, most people find their free time goes down considerably, and without unstructured free time, it's harder to form natural bonds with new people. If you've found your circle has gotten significantly smaller, or perhaps you've moved to a new town recently, or realize that you're lonely and would like to build more healthy, meaningful friendships, then try inviting someone to a playdate. You might just find someone who's just as eager as you to build a great, new friendship with.

Summary: A key foundational element for building a meaningful life is the ability to build authentic connections with others. We might learn these pieces of these adaptive skills in our early years, have them deconstructed through the cutthroat adolescent years, and hopefully integrate them into our relationships by the time we're adults- but don't count on it. Relationship skills must be cultivated and nurtured. Can you imagine healthy friendships without them?

26 How do you care for your friends?
EMPATHETIC LISTENING

I'll never forget the feeling I had when I was packing up my dorm room to move home for the summer after my freshman year in college. I was going around to knock on the doors of my neighbors to say goodbye and share contact info with them with promises to stay in touch over the summer. One kid two doors down made a simple comment that he might not be coming back the following year. I remember that I felt...nothing. He could've told me that he was going to the dentist that afternoon and I would've felt the same- nothing.

I went back to my dorm to finish packing my bags and then it hit me- I have no friends here. Not really. No one that I really know, and no one who really knows me. That kid was the person I had spent the most time with during that year, and here he was telling me that we might never see each other again and I couldn't care less if I was honest. It was probably the loneliest moment of my life.

The reality sunk in on my drive home to my parent's house that if I didn't return to school the next year nobody would miss me. Not really. And I wouldn't miss them. That was so far from the college experience I thought I would have, and so far from the experience I imagined my high school friends having at their respective schools. I just couldn't let that be my reality. I vowed to return the following year with a different mindset.

I committed to learning how to grow true friendships.

When you're little, you can get away with not being a good friend. For most people, like me, your close relationships are formed by convenience. The kids who live on your block, the kids on your team, the kids in your class. But when you grow up, you can no longer rely on proximity or playdates set up by mom. By nature, we start selecting friendships based on the quality of the person and the quality of the relationship. It becomes critically important that we learn to build friendships- a skill that is never taught in school and typically not modeled for us well by our parents.

And, if we could simplify friendship building down to one important skill above all else, it would be the ability to listen with an empathetic posture. Empathetic listening is the grounding for real, authentic connection and shared experience. It's what helps people feel seen, known, and understood. It's what helps us feel safe, cared for, and supported.

So what is empathetic listening, and how do we teach it? Building authentic friendships of belonging are the foundation for building a meaningful life, and it deserves as much concentrated education and training as we would put into an AP Physics exam or college application (or more!).

7 Uncommon Sense Tips for Empathic Listening

1. **Un-distracted attention**: One of the most subtle and worst things anyone can do in a conversation is to glance at their phones or watch. I remember going to a therapist early in my 20's and he would look at his watch and yawn. The message: I am not here, buddy.

2. **Hold your surprise:** I don't need you to agree with or understand what I'm saying, but when you act shocked my internal radar screams: "Stop sharing- not safe!". Empathetic listening means you withhold your surprise and seek to understand better.

3. **Listen underneath**: Empathetic listening is about listening to more than just words being spoken. It's an intentional interpreting of facial expressions, emotion, and underlying beliefs or thoughts. It's an active pursuit to understand what's not being said as much as what is.

4. **Play the mirror**: When someone else is sharing something, one of the most helpful ways to communicate that you're present and that you care is to mirror their emotions and facial expressions. More than just an improv warmup technique, it helps someone feel safe to share more.

5. **Shut your mouth**: Most of the time, all a person needs is to be heard or know you're there. You don't need to talk.

6. **Check yourself:** Ask questions to make sure you understand and aren't interpreting what someone else is sharing from your own lens or perspective. Questions like, "What do you mean?", "Why do you think it happened like that?", or "Tell me more about...".

7. **Circle back**: If you want to really help someone feel cared for, supported, and valuable, then circle back with them in a day or a week to let them know you're still thinking about what they shared. It will show them that you were present, that you remember, and that you're a trustworthy and ongoing presence in their lives.

Each one of those uncommon sense tips is an intentional practice anyone can learn to do. Empathy isn't a gift reserved for a few talented nurturing types. Anyone can learn it, and every kid should be given the opportunity to learn how.

Summary: A key foundational element for building a meaningful life is practicing empathetic listening. Authentic relationships go both ways, and it would be extremely difficult to build good ones without this skill. You might be able to add to the depth of your friendships through acts of service, constant presence, or a calm demeanor, but unless you learn to hold space and listen to their mind and heart, you'll be missing out.

27 How do you repair relationships?
CONFLICT RESOLUTION SKILLS

One of the most significant moments I've had with a friend came because we had a fight. Just a few days after graduating from college, my friend, John, and I were hanging out in someone's backyard having a BBQ and pool party. I said something sarcastic and silly and accidentally sprayed him with a hose. He responded quickly, saying something like- "Dude- you're so dumb". His tone was intense. My feelings were hurt. It all happened so quickly.

A few minutes later, as I was changing in the bathroom I had a little discussion with myself. I realized that my feelings were really hurt- John had been a good friend, and I really, really didn't like what he said or how he said it. It occurred to me there and then that this was an inflection moment. My subconscious was telling me this was the time to push away and not be close friends anymore. I wanted to protect myself.

But then, I felt something else. I felt sad. I didn't want to dissolve our friendship- John was becoming such a close friend- like a brother to me. But the only model I'd ever seen before from my family was when you get annoyed or irritated with a friend- you move on. Never talk again. Find a new friend. I didn't want to do that, though. And yet, I knew I couldn't pretend like my feelings weren't hurt. It was too significant. I had to address the conflict.

I left the bathroom and approached John awkwardly. With as much courage as I could muster, I looked at him and said something like, "Man, what you said really hurt my feelings. I didn't mean to spray you with the hose. I know I was acting sarcastic, and I'm sorry about that. But I really didn't like what you said or how you said it." I don't think I took a breath at all and just stood there and stared at him.

Here's the part I'll never forget. John looked at me for a few seconds and then broke into a huge grin. He said, "Do you realize what's happening right now? We're having our first fight! I've only have had fights and arguments with my brothers, never with a friend. This is awesome!" Then, he apologized, and we both laughed. We still laugh about it.

That was twenty years ago. He's been like a brother ever since.

I can't imagine how much richness I would've missed if we hadn't resolved that little conflict twenty years ago. His friendship means the world to me, and it's not the only time we've had to address conflict with each other over the years.

Conflict is awkward. Uncomfortable. Distressing. Overwhelming. Vulnerable. But on the other side of it is all the good stuff- connection, intimacy, commitment, support, and love.

We want every kid to have every opportunity to build a meaningful life, a life that's rich, and deep, and filled with love. So, we have to teach kids how to resolve conflict. It's not something that you just pick up. It has to be deliberately modeled, trained and affirmed. By us.

Here are seven uncommon sense principles for conflict resolution:

1. **Recognize there's conflict**: the first step to resolving conflict is actually recognizing that there's a break in the relationship. This part is subtle- I'm always tempted to act or pretend or convince myself that nothing's really wrong. But, the more self-aware and honest I become, the more I'm able to recognize when something's been damaged and needs repair.

2. **Read the story underneath the story**: renowned researcher, author, and speaker Brené Brown shared a pro-tip- whenever our feelings get triggered, our brains are wired to make sense of what we're feeling with a story we invent, and it's usually a negative story. For instance, let's say a friend shows up late to meet you for lunch. Subconsciously, we invent a story that our friend has more important things to do than spend time with us. Or, our friend isn't a real friend- they're selfish and chaotic. Either of those stories may or may not be true, but believing them causes a rift in the relationship.

3. **Own your part:** in my experience, it's pretty rare for a conflict to be completely one-sided. I'd say 98% of the time, it takes two to tango. It might be that you have a deep-seated belief that being

early means you're a good person. Or, it might be that you knew their previous commitment might make it challenging to get there on time, but because the time worked better for your schedule, you pushed for it.

4. **Take initiative**: one of the key parts of resolving conflict is the willingness to make a move towards the other person. I know- it's probably all their fault. They should make the first move. But, experience shows that if you're willing to make the first move, everything will go better. It might look like this- start by sending a text or mention over the phone, "Remind me to bring up something about lunch the other day when we see each other tomorrow."

5. **Share your experience, own your feelings**: I'm sure you've heard this before- the notion that you should share your feelings with "I feel..." statements. Well, do you know why you've heard that so often before? Because it works! It also helps if you take Brené's advice and share the story that you invented in your mind about what happened. Give them a chance to respond to your story.

6. **Listen for understanding**: the next hardest part is to give the other person the opportunity to respond and share their feelings and their experience. It's hard because they might not respond the way you hope. They might have hurt feelings, too. They might have a perspective that's difficult to hear. They might bring up old wounds. They might shut down and not respond at all. This is the point of your most significant surrender.

7. **Commit to repairing**: finally, if you get this far and both of you had the chance to share your feelings and perspective, it's an

opportunity to talk through ways to repair the relationship and avoid repeating the same patterns. It might be an apology and a hug. It might look like a commitment to show up on time, or be more honest with each other earlier. It might even be taking some space for a while to allow yourselves some time to work through your feelings. Or, perhaps, this is the time to shift the dynamics of the friendship.

It's difficult to imagine someone going through life and building authentic, supportive relationships- the kind that everyone wants and everyone needs in order to thrive, without learning how to practice conflict resolution. What are the other options? Shallow friendships where we avoid getting too close? Shutting down friendships and moving on when things get uncomfortable or awkward?

Resolving conflict isn't for the faint of heart. It's not easy and it's incredibly vulnerable. But on the other side of a conflict is a deeper connection, more substantial commitment, and a more meaningful life. It's worth it; we have to teach our kids how to resolve conflict.

Summary: A key foundational element for building a meaningful life is learning conflict resolution skills. The quality and depth of your relationships are contingent upon learning how to resolve conflict- and they are learnable skills as well as commitments and values. If you haven't grown up watching adults resolve conflict in healthy ways, you'll need to try even harder to find good examples and role models to show you what it looks like. Once you do, though, your friendships will never be the same.

28 How do you connect with others who are different?
CROSS-CULTURAL SKILLS

The first and most profound memory I have of a cultural faux pas was my first day of high school. I followed my older sister's footsteps by going to the new private Catholic school in our community. Having never stepped foot into a church before, the first day all students were invited to the 'Welcome Mass' in the gym- a full-on liturgical event with incense, priests in robes, and music I'd never heard before. It was all completely overwhelming. The worst part came more than halfway through the service. Suddenly hundreds of students were standing up and getting in line to slowly and solemnly walk down the bleacher stairs to the man in the robe. Trying to fit in and follow along, I stood up and got in line, not knowing any protocol or etiquette or requirements for receiving what I know now is called the Eucharist. I was peering over their shoulders and sneaking a peek down to the front of the line where in my shock I saw fellow students grabbing what looked like food or a cracker or a mini Nilla wafer and eating it. I marched forward, grabbed my share, put it in my mouth, and found my place again.

A couple of hours later when I got home I confronted my sister. "Hey, thanks a lot for the heads up on the rituals today. You gave me no warning! I ate a flavorless cracker and I'm pretty sure I'm supposed to get baptized tomorrow!" She was shocked, no doubt called me an idiot like only an older sibling can do, and I felt even more humiliated.

In this life, you cannot avoid crossing cultures. Really, any time you leave the house you'll cross cultures. Every family has their own, every ethnicity, race, religion, and neighborhood has it, too. When a kid goes to school they cross cultures, and when they go to work someday they will be there, too.

You can't avoid it being uncomfortable, either. If you learn to do it well, life will go better for you. You will build stronger social connections. You'll grow in empathy and understanding. You will grow in confidence in your own identity. You will be able to learn from others and experience a richer life. It's a key ingredient to building a meaningful life.

Here are some uncommon sense principles for learning to adapt to a different culture and build connections with people who are different than you (acknowledging that I'm writing from a white male perspective):

- **Choose your mindset**: if you enter the situation with suspicion, self-centeredness, prejudice, or fear, it's not going to go well. If you choose to be open, humble, curious, and trusting- it will go way better.
- **Find an interpreter**: crossing cultures can be disorienting. Your perception, values, and language code will be misinterpreted, and

vice versa. It helps if you can recruit someone who will show you the way to understanding. Call that person an interpreter or a tour guide, obviously, they don't speak for everyone but an insider can help you make sense of how to decode and engage more effectively.

- **Stay on your toes**: as soon as you get complacent, you forget the cultural differences. Becoming comfortable is a good thing, but it's always helpful to stay on your toes and intentionally choose to be open, curious, and engaging.
- **Recognize when you need to take a lap or take a breath**: we all respond differently to the tension and discomfort of cultural dissonance. Some people will want to 'turtle' and protect themselves. Others will poke or project or critique. Either way, it's not helpful. Cultural competency requires consistent, intentional engagement. If you stay the course and stay open, you'll find new levels of understanding and depth. It's helpful to remember that you can take a step back, check with your heart, check with a friend, and then reengage.

Life is filled with moments of cultural dissonance. Every time your kid goes to school, they experience the conflict of crossing cultures. When they play on a team, they need to adapt to that culture. When they go off to college, they'll cross cultures. When they work someday, they'll need to learn to adjust to a new culture. When they travel, when they interact with a neighbor, and when they get married- they'll be crossing cultures.

For some, cultural competencies are a necessary survival skill. For others, especially coming from a dominant culture, this conversation will probably require some guidance, facilitation, and intentional displacement. Regardless, cultural competency is not a nice thing to have- it's a necessity for every kid to be able to engage and to thrive in this life.

Summary: A key foundational element for building a meaningful life is learning to develop connections with people who are different than you. You can deliberately try to avoid spending time with people who come from different backgrounds or have different perspectives than you, but you'll be unsuccessful. In fact, through a broad perspective, everyone outside of your immediate family comes from a culture different from your own, so learning how to adapt, understand, and even adopt other cultural values and norms will be crucial for anyone to build authentic connections.

29 How do you best contribute to a team?
COLLABORATION SKILLS

Do you remember the worst part about being in school- more than the soggy nuggets in the cafeteria or the repetitive worksheets or the annoying kid you sat next to? Everyone, say it with me now: "Group Projects!". Group projects were the worst!

I'll never forget as a high school senior our history teacher was beyond excited to spearhead a new program to our school- it was kind of like the science fair meets social studies. We were assigned to a team and supposed to pick an area of interest we could all agree upon (yeah, right) and then do a massive deep dive into the content to come up with a unique perspective in the form of a presentation. And, of course, even though we were given the entire semester to work on the project together, guess what we did? Just like every other team- we waited until the last minute. It's still the only time besides when my wife was in labor that I pulled an all-nighter. I don't even remember what topic we chose.

Do you know what I learned from that experience? You might assume nothing, but I learned this vital lesson that I've tried to unlearn ever since- group projects suck!

But just because you finish school doesn't mean you graduate from group projects- whether it's being on a team at work, serving on the PTA, or planning a family reunion. I've been on countless teams over the past twenty years of work. Even now I am a part of at least a half dozen different teams. I can't escape them! Fortunately, each time I get a little better at participating in a helpful way, knowing my role, adapting to others, engaging in healthy conflict, and working towards a goal.

Imagine, though, if instead of the final presentation being the point of the Social Studies / Science Fair, the learning was focused on group dynamics? What if we were deliberately taught how to be on a team in an effective way? To learn the different roles people play, even to be assigned to play those different parts and then reflect on the experience. Those are lessons I would've actually remembered.

We all tend to play different roles when we participate on a team. At an early age, we can start helping our kids become effective teammates, become more self-aware, and learn how to collaborate well with others. It starts by giving honest, neutral observations of what we see in them from the way they interact with others. We can also ask them to make observations about the other people on their team- who does what and how that affects the others. We can remind them throughout their growing up years that teams and collaboration are a central part of life, encouraging them to keep learning and keep leaning in.

- *What have you learned about collaborating with others?*
- *What lessons would you want your kids to learn about serving on a team?*

Summary: A key foundational element for building a meaningful life is learning to collaborate well with others. You just can't do well in life-family, friendship, or work without it. People are inherently complex, dynamic, and multi-layered, which is why our skillset for working well with them needs to be adaptive, too. Learning collaboration skills will help you be successful in all areas of your life.

29 How do you come across to others?
GROWING IN SOCIAL-AWARENESS

One of the bizarre aspects of parenting that no one prepares you for is watching the same movies again and again and again and again until every line is memorized. Most of the time, it's mind-numbing to watch the movies the first time, much less the ninth time. But every now and then my kids fall in love with a film that captures my heart, too.

Disney's Tangled is the animated story of Rapunzel- based loosely on the German fairy tale by the Brothers Grimm. In the original story, Rapunzel is sought after by a prince. In Disney's version, Rapunzel is ignited to go on her own exploration of self-discovery, to explore who she is and where she comes from. She intuitively knows that there's more to herself than she's been told, and enlists a boy-bandit named Flynn Rider to guide her. The rest of the movie is about Rapunzel's journey to discover where she came from and who she really is.

Daniel Goleman is the godfather of learning about yourself, especially as it relates to management and organizational health. He said, "If your emotional abilities aren't in hand, if you don't have self-awareness, if you are not able to manage your distressing emotions, if you can't have empathy and have effective relationships, then no matter how smart you are, you are not going to get very far." Coining the term EQ (Emotional Intelligence), Goleman almost single-handedly changed the public perception about self-discovery, and the management industry has jumped on his bandwagon. Harvard Professor of Cognition and Education Howard Gardner said, "The less a person understands his own feelings, the more he will fall prey to them. The less a person understands the feelings, the responses, and the behavior of others, the more likely he will interact inappropriately with them and therefore fail to secure his proper place in the world." It's become normal to get to know yourself.

But, the self-discovery journey is a long one. Despite its accepted value, most people have never taken the opportunity to explore the insides of who they are, where they've come from, or how they come across to others. It's complex, overwhelming, and takes a really long time and a lot of energy. The journey doesn't really have an end. And there are haters every step of the way. People convincing you to quit being so "self-consumed". People's eyes glazing over when you start talking about the deeper parts of you. Derogatory names like "navel-glazer" or narcissist.

Like Rapunzel, though, I think there's something deep inside all of us that calls out to explore the deep. People who've traveled there report profound freedom that comes from self-acceptance, find deeper satisfaction in their choices and feel confident forging their own path. Every journey starts with a single step, as well as a decision to keep at it. But after you make the decision you're also going to need to know which steps to take.

Four Uncommon Sense Steps to Learning About Yourself

- Constantly assume there's more to you than meets the eye
- Identify and sit with the right questions
- Get feedback from the right people
- Spend time with the right guide

The single most important thing adults who work with kids can do to help them grow into self-awareness is provide opportunities for them to be reflective on their inner and external worlds. We can prompt them to explore what's going on inside, and how external variables influence them- and vice versa. We can give them a few moments to think, both on their own and out loud.

We can also serve as a mirror to them, reflecting back on what we see and observe about who they are and how they come across. Too often we assume that students know how they come across. They don't. And if they are thinking about it, typically their mirror is distorted by their own insecurities or ego. When we realize that, we can step into our role as adults who guide them into more self-awareness, without an agenda other than helping them become the best version of themselves.

Summary: A key foundational element for building a meaningful life is learning how you come across to others. Social awareness is a core competency of emotional intelligence, enabling you to adapt how you're relating to and communicating with people who are different from you. It's what allows you to adjust your communication style so you can find shared meaning, deliver and receive accurate messages. It's a key part of building authentic, healthy friendships that will last.

30 Who guides you?
PERSONAL MENTORS

Luke had Yoda. Frodo had Gandalf. Elastigirl had Edna. Martin Luther King, Jr. had Benjamin Mays. Kobe had MJ.

Every significant person in history and every important character in a story had a guide, someone to develop their talents and steer them into their full potential.

Who's your guide?

In college I met a man named Chris who advised a student leadership organization I joined. At first I didn't quite know what to do with him—honestly I hadn't spent much time with adults who weren't in my family, or teachers, or sports coaches. Chris was interesting, and funny, and people were drawn to him. And for some reason, he was drawn to me. I remember when we first met for coffee- I'd never met anyone for coffee before and didn't even drink it. We met for an hour, and Chris probably asked me three dozen questions about my life. I doubt I asked him any about his.

I liked it.

He was interested in me. He made me laugh, and feel comfortable. He helped me think through a few areas of my life, and pulled a few ideas out of my head and articulate things I hadn't really thought of before. I knew he liked me, and I definitely liked being around him.

Over the next few years I drank a lot of coffee with Chris. I learned that he was a great person to go to when I had questions- about my major, about girls, and even about my parent's divorce. I also learned that he saw things in me that I hadn't seen before.

Correction: he saw things in me that I always wished someone else saw in me. Things that were deep down- attributes of my character and hints of talent that no one had recognized or pointed out or called out of invited me into. He got me on the good path, the right path for my life.

So, who's your Guide?

Whom do you trust? Who's the person that you can turn to when you have deep, relevant, perplexing questions about your life and Life? Who do you know that really inspires you, who lives focused on making an impact and making a difference, someone you can model your life after?

When I had to make a decision about what to do with my life after college, I knew I had a lot of options. I could follow the footsteps of my family members before me and go into finance. I could break out on my own and go into real estate. I could follow a dormant dream of mine and become a High School English teacher. I chose to follow Chris. He invited me to work for his company and learn to become who I was supposed to become- an influencer, a speaker, a leader.

Chris was the one who saw it in me. He was the one who challenged me when I was disengaged. He affirmed me in public and told me what I could be great at. Before I met him I was on a different path, and in many ways I can say my life is entirely different because I spent time with him. But as I look back, all he did was to help me get on the path I was always supposed to be on.

I'm really glad I said yes to that coffee.

At the YouSchool, we believe a Guide is the essential ingredient for everyone to live their best lives, their right story. That's why we work with the best people on the planet- people who love students, who have a ton of experience working with them, and most importantly, have the character and dimension to be able to develop potential in others. They've already done a lot of their own growth, and now want to pour into others.

Do you have a Guide?

Summary: no one is successful in life in any endeavor on their own. Not only do they need a supportive cast of characters, but most importantly, they need someone who will show them the way. It's impossible to imagine someone living a meaningful life without a trusted guide. Chances are, you'll have multiple Guides throughout your life in different areas. You might have a career guide- someone who can show you the way. You might have a marriage and family guide- someone who can model, demonstrate, and point out the ways you can align your values to how you interact with your family. In other words, you need help; everyone does.

WRAPPING UP: BELONGING

I skipped a LOT of school days in the 4th grade. Being pretty good at acting (a.k.a. lying), I convinced my mom that I was getting chronic, severe headaches. Nope. In reality, I had a lot of social anxiety and didn't have the tools or the confidence to push through.

Then came middle school. Since my Ferris Bueller headache ruse had been uncovered, I didn't have school absences to fall back on. I had to go. But the social anxiety was way worse. The threats were so much higher! Actual rejection, physical harm, and intimidation. Comparison between developed or non-developing bodies- it was all so painful.

We all have a story about getting picked last for the kickball team in P.E. class back in the day. The experiences of rejection stay with us for a long time, imprinting memories on us that can undermine a lot throughout our lives. The need to fit in, be accepted, and feel like you belong for who you truly are is a profoundly human experience. Our kids feel it more than we do, and if we as parents and educators can keep that in mind, we will be better equipped to guide them to a thriving life.

Erik Erikson is known as the father of adult development. He was a psychologist who coined the phrase, 'identity crisis', and helped us understand the developmental stages we all go through on the way to adulthood. He said the primary challenge for adolescents is to create a healthy personal identity as well as healthy peer relationships- two dynamics often at odds with each other.

Fitting in is a process that we try to manage for our kids when they are little. We want them to wear the proper, in-fashion clothing at preschool and eat the best diet. We want them to avoid embarrassment or harassment on the playground. But when they reach the middle school years, they take over the management of fitting in on their own terms. As their brains wake up to self-consciousness, they also shift the focus of their security away from their caregivers towards their peers. They are quite literally looking at their peers as a stand-in mirror- to help them get an impression of themselves, who they are, and how they're measured. One dangerous part of this process is a kid might make unhealthy choices to use harmful substances in their quest to be accepted by their peers.

Here's the problem: the desire to **fit in** is actually not the goal. What we want to do is feel like we **belong**. The difference is when we fit in we learn to sacrifice or hide some important parts of ourselves to be able to blend in and be accepted rather than rejected. True belonging, however, comes when we are accepted because of our uniqueness and differences. It's not until we truly own our quirky selves, our preferences, our interests, and our quirks- and disclose them to others that we can experience what we really hope for deep down.

Of course, adolescence is so much about exploration and discovery. We don't yet know ourselves so we need to try on different personas to see how they resonate or not. We need to try different values and adopt different views to see if they work for us. We are searching for a life that is both intrinsically consistent with who we are and aspirational for who we want to become.

As parents and educators, the most helpful thing we can offer is affirmation and support as kids go through this discovery process. We can be accurate mirrors to help them see themselves clearly. We can invite them to reflect on their choices and persona to help them learn more effectively about themselves. We can offer compassion and grace when they get off track and be patient as they try to figure things out for themselves. More than anything, we can continue to accept them for who they are, even if who they are is different than what we want for them or see in them. We can give them an experience of belonging through a relationship with us, which is incredibly valuable as they make their way in the world.

A life without experiences of true belonging is a life without love. Can you imagine someone who has a clear identity and a compelling purpose but doesn't have people to share life with? Of course not, that would be miserable.

If we're going to emphasize one of the three big pillars, it must be belonging. If you think about it the other way, if someone has love in their life through rich relationships, but is still figuring out their identity and hasn't yet found a compelling purpose, they still have love. A life without love is not much of a life at all.

PART ONE CONCLUSION:
The Purpose of Adolescence

Around the age of 13 kids start becoming more self-aware. It comes across, actually, more like what I'd call self-consciousness. You begin noticing yourself, your body, the way your voice sounds, the way others interact with you and respond to you, and you are hyper-aware of what your peers are doing, saying, and looking like. The primary objective is self-preservation- avoid shame and humiliation and rejection at all costs by your tribe, your pack, your peers. Some kids are better at it than others, some have it easier than others. But every kid goes through it.

I remember always wanting to dress like the older cool boys on my street. They wore Quiksilver t-shirts and O.P. corduroy shorts when I was really little, but my mom dressed me in tucked-in polos and khaki shorts. She still defends her style choices for me, by the way, and will until the day she dies. I remember overhearing a kid talk about the Power 106 radio station when I got to Middle School and listening for the first time to hip hop and gangsta rap. I don't know if I genuinely liked the music or just wanted to give the impression that I was into what other kids were into. A kid on the bus one day told me about a radio show called Love Line that was on every night after 10 pm and they'd take calls from regular people about sex and relationships. I had to sneak a radio under my bed and earphones to listen to it so I could laugh along with the jokes the following day with the other kids.

When we're really little, it's our parents who act as the mirrors and interpreters of reality for us. They tell us who we are and who we belong to- through their eye contact and cuddling and cutting the crust off of our sandwiches. Our extended family lets us know that we're loved and cherished just for being alive and in the family, and we know we're safe and sound.

But then we go to Middle School. Our brains wake up and undergo tremendous restructuring. There's fewer adults around than ever, and we start the long process of self-discovery and life construction that many people never productively work through.

There are three significant, monumental shifts happening throughout adolescence:

1. Kids want to separate themselves from the people they come from and discover their own unique identity
2. Kids want to understand what value they have to the world
3. Kids want to find people who will love and accept them not because they have to but because they're lovable

Kids want to separate themselves. They pull away from the people they come from and go on an undefined quest to discover their own unique identity. Every kid does this, and it can feel terrifying to a parent (talking about myself here). We did it, too. We pulled away from the adults in our life and looked to other kids to help us understand who we are and how the world works. If you consider this long enough, you might realize what a ridiculous idea this is: *"I'm going to pull away from the people in my life who actually have some life wisdom, actually see me for who I really am, and instead go try to get all of my answers from a bunch of other teenagers."*

When my son was in elementary school we started an almost nightly routine of taking a walk around the neighborhood together after his younger sisters went to bed. He's a night owl and has no problem waking up early in the morning. It was our special time together- he would ask me all afternoon and all throughout dinner if we could take a walk together and then as soon as we started walking he'd beg to go farther than we went the night before and stay out later. He would talk my ear off, asking non-stop question after question about every topic he could imagine. I loved our walks. But then, he started Middle School. And he stopped asking me for the walks, almost overnight. And I started asking him to go with me. Usually, he'd politely decline. When we did take a walk, it was a short one. We didn't talk much. I became the one asking the questions. But not too many- his answers were always pretty short. I can remember many walks saying to myself, "This is normal. This is normal. This is healthy. This is normal." Honestly, I felt sad, and lonely, and anxious that my little buddy was gone. I found myself a few times, out of my sadness and grief and anxiety poking at him, hoping to get a reaction out of him. It was hard to let go.

Kids want to understand what value they have to the rest of the world. Kids who live in families without much stress or trauma, with consistent parental figures will have a deep foundation of love, acceptance, and belonging. They know they have value because they're shown that from day one. But during adolescence, it doesn't matter as much anymore that their primary family thinks they're special. They want to test their specialness out in the world. They want to get the affirmation that who they are and what they have is valuable, significant, and essential. They're looking for feedback that lets them know their life matters and will matter. They're looking for ways to contribute, opportunities to solve problems, and for the validation of their unique wiring.

I remember going to my first job as a 'Sandwich Artist' at a local deli. My parents expected me to get a job over summer and I had a family connection with the owner who was kind enough to give me a chance. I'd never scrambled an egg before, or had a conversation with an adult outside my family or school, or even played with a toy cash register as a kid. I was utterly unqualified in terms of skill, and I was terrified. In hindsight, it was the perfect opportunity for a first job. I had to learn how to talk with adults, handle stress calmly, listen effectively, and be productive. There was no way I could get by with the bare minimum, and throughout the summer months I learned how to make good sandwiches and greet customers like a seasoned pro (pun intended). Even with the tiny paychecks I received earning $4.50/hour, I earned validation that I could contribute to something valuable, even as small as lunch. It was the first of many summer jobs where I got accurate feedback from adults outside my family that I had something to offer.

Kids want to find people who will love them. They need to find people who will love and accept them not because they have to but as a family obligation, but because they're lovable in and of themselves. They have inherent worth, freely chosen by others expressed through loyalty, interdependence, laughter, and generosity. Your mom and your grandma can tell you millions of times how lovable you are, but it's not until you experience that love manifested through friends that you start to believe a little bit of the words they shared.

Nic was in my freshman drama class and it was love at first sight between us. We just hit it off immediately- same sense of humor, similar outlook towards high school, plus a shared interest in getting the attention of girls. I had lots of friends until that point but Nic was different. Since the beginning, he's been genuinely interested in me- my thoughts, my ideas, my perspective, my questions, and the path that I'm on in life. It continues now over twenty five years later and he's one of the core reminders in my life of my inherent worth and value. I know I'm okay because I have him in my life and by my side.

PART TWO: RETHINKING WHAT KIDS NEED

It Takes One to Know One

In P.D. Eastman's classic tale, *Are You My Mother*, he tells the story about a freshly hatched bird who goes on a search for his mother. The book is more than an engaging kid's story, it's a fable about identity formation- how we all search for accurate mirrors to help us both understand who we are and how to live well in this world. Everywhere the bird turns, from farm animal to tractor, he's left with the same answer: "*Nope!*". It's not until he finds his real mother that he considers an accurate mirror that gives him the security for who he really is.

We partner with school leaders, teachers and parents to reshape school culture so that all students build meaningful, fulfilling lives. We offer consulting, training, and curriculum, but no matter how effective we are there is one vital ingredient that is essential: healthy adults flourishing in their own lives and modeling that kind of life to kids.

The ongoing challenge is to communicate an uncomfortable yet straightforward truth to teachers in schools and parents at home, many of who are overworked, overstressed, and overwhelmed. Your primary expectation is to develop kids into flourishing adults, and your primary responsibility is to live the kind of life you want kids to live, too. As much as you need to provide for your kids (parents), teach content to students or manage their activities, if you lose focus on thriving in your own meaningful, fulfilling life you cannot give kids what they need.

The best research out there on healthy emerging adulthood says each kid needs to have positive, interactive relationships with **at least five adults through their teen years**. Those adults can model and demonstrate what authentic living looks like from different perspectives. No one adult bears the burden of all the responsibility to be a kid's end-all and be-all, though. Kids are smart enough to pull different aspects from different people and create their own version of how life can work. As kids experiment with and search for answers to life's big questions, the adults in their lives act as mirrors that reflect what their beliefs, values, engagement, and relationships might look like in the flesh. If they don't get to see those things in adults, they'll likely continue to wonder what it could look like. They'll keep searching for clarity and conviction well past the years that would serve them the most.

Adults involved with kids must show them what good living looks like:

They need to model humility and own their mistakes.

They need to engage in healthy friendships of mutual belonging.

They have to show how to express personal beliefs and convictions.

They must put others first.

They need to show personal growth, and emotional intelligence.

They can show kids what self-acceptance looks like.

They can model for kids what it means to take responsibility for their weaknesses.

They can show why engaging with your past trauma or confronting your addictions will lead to better living.

This all makes sense, right? Like kids used to say: It takes one to know one. We won't raise kids to become flourishing adults living meaningful, fulfilling lives until and unless they see what it looks like first. It's a lot like the rules of math, and it's a problem we're aiming to solve.

A Process To Clarify Their Life's Story

In high school, students are encouraged to choose good colleges to apply to. It's universally understood that going to a good school will unlock opportunities for you to succeed later on in life. Conventional wisdom says that in college you can "find yourself"- discover who you are, what you're good at, what you enjoy, and get on track to a meaningful career. If you don't know who you are in High School, don't worry- you'll get to that soon.

In college, students are encouraged early to get onto a career track by selecting a major. For some schools, students have to pick an education track as they apply to the school, even before they get there. Of course, there are a lot of students who delay that decision, or change their minds at least once, but eventually you have to either drop out of college, or graduate. If you haven't "found yourself" by the end of college, don't worry- that's what you can do when you get a job.

I remember being a Junior in college headed quickly towards my Senior year and realizing that I wasn't very confident about the path I was on. I was an Accounting major, but the idea of a long career in Accounting didn't sound overly thrilling, even if it was stable and secure. Starting my Senior year, I had a moment where I just knew I couldn't go down that path. With the help of a few good conversations with friends, circumstances and other opportunities, I realized that I wanted to do something else with my life and even become someone else than the trajectory I was on.

What do you do when you want to figure out who you are, and quickly?

The problem is there is no app for that. Well, actually, there is! Personality and aptitude tests are delivered on an app on your phone that can literally tell you who you are. There are apps for figuring yourself out. If you don't have the app, there are a few other conventional ways people go about figuring themselves out:

- The **'Tell-Me-Who-I-Am Approach'**: give me a test, and show me the results
- The **'Common-Sense Approach'**: take a good look at my skills, education, and experience, then extrapolate forward. If you studied Accounting, are good at math, look good with a suit on, then…
- The **'I've-Known-Since-I-Was-4 Approach'**: the kid who wanted to be a Doctor who is pre-med in college, gets great grades, aces the MCAT, and never looks back
- The **'Get-Lucky Approach'**: the Lebron James, I know I'm amazing and a recruiter will call me any day now to tell me

what phenomenal opportunity they customized for me approach

The problem with the 'Tell-Me-Who-I-Am Approach' is that I know I'm way more complicated than any test can tell me, so the results don't stick. The 'Common-Sense Approach' is what most people do- most bored, disengaged, unexciting people. If you're still reading this it means you don't fit into the The 'I've-Known-Since-I-Was-4 Approach'. And, the 'Get-Lucky Approach' just might work out, any second now...

What if there was an ACTUAL, PROVEN PROCESS that could help you discover who you are, what makes you tick, and how to live the life you're meant to live?

A few years ago, we started to pay attention to a huge, universal problem. We found 90% of students were graduating top universities without any clear sense of who they were. 100% of them wanted to live an extraordinary life, do something meaningful, live a great story with their lives, and be happy. But only 10% felt confident that they were on the right path.

So we got to work. First, we looked at the different Approaches (see above). Then, with a few hypotheses, we began testing a common-sense, discovery-based process that could get young people to self-awareness, self-confidence, and self-direction. Quickly.

Nick Saban, head coach of Alabama's football team, is famous (read: notorious) for his 'Process'. Players in his program get indoctrinated into step-by-step thinking- every position matters, every play matters, and every piece of the play matters. Coach Saban says, "Rather than focusing on the outcome, focus on the process." His genius, and continuous success, is knowing that focusing on outcomes gets you trapped in a cycle of stress, pressure and fear- terrible ingredients for getting consistent high performance. Rather, focusing on the process and evaluating on the process helps you focus, and the results come.

The YouSchool curriculum is the process for people to cut through the stress, pressure, and fear that is at play in life transition and get to clarity.

We built the process, we tested the process, and we refined the process. When people in transition engage in our approach, they get to clarity. They say things like:

"Now I know who I am, who I want to be, and what to do with my life."

If quite literally everyone wants their life to tell a great story, both about the kinds of people they are and the accomplishments they create, then it's time for a new approach. One that works.

Guided Wisdom

If you haven't seen your teen or your students act foolishly lately- just wait a minute. It's gonna happen. Teenagers are notorious for making poor choices. They often act impulsively without any concern for long-term consequences. Sometimes, like one of our kids recently, they make foolish choices that have massive consequences.

It's not their fault- it's developmentally where they're at. Teens are motivated to find acceptance. They have very little life experience to draw from. Their pre-frontal cortex (the part of the brain that authors rational thought and executive functioning) is unformed. They lack the ability to consider alternatives or contingencies or implications.

Too often, though, we dismiss the ongoing learning opportunities readily available for every teen with a "kids will be kids" attitude. It's not their fault, but it's our opportunity to teach them and train them to be better prepared for building a meaningful life.

So how do we help teenagers become more conscious, more aware, and wiser?

1. **Never waste an opportunity**: the best part of every Full House episode was the last 90 seconds when the soft mood music would start and Danny Tanner (R.I.P.!) would have a heart-to-heart with Stephanie or DJ. While we might not have a soundtrack to play, we can look for moments to talk through certain problems or issues AFTER the big emotions or conflict have subsided.

2. **Share your own stories:** I know you did some dumb stuff back in the day, too. We all did. So rather than hide those stories in fear that they'll follow your example, be an authentic role model, and share everything with them (at appropriate ages and stages), especially the lessons you learned in hindsight.

3. **Always ask 'why':** one of the most consistent conflicts parents and children have is around one central idea: *"Why did you do that?"* Typically, what we mean when we ask that question is a little less subtle: "You are a dummy!" They feel that vibe from us, and rather than having a productive, TGIF parent moment with our kid, they act defensively to avoid your shame. Instead, after the emotions have subsided, we can inquire in tangential ways: "So tell me, when you started to skateboard down the hill, were you wondering if you might fall?" Or, "Before you snuck out of the house, did you have a plan for what would happen if you got caught?" We can ask them why they did what they did, give them time to consider their actions and choices, and keep asking them to be thoughtful and reflective. Maybe, just maybe, one day they'll think...before they act.

Pointing Out the Positive

As a parent of three kids, I have plenty to complain about. The insults, slights, and affronts are rampant in our home- just like every home. We all bounce off of each other- our insecurities, annoyances, and pet peeves. We can easily irritate each other and bring out the worst in each other. Some days are more complicated than others, especially those days where we spend a lot of time together like on a weekend or a vacation.

It can be difficult on those days to find any goodness in our kids, and if you're anything like me, my temptation is to lean away from them, to get away from them and get some alone time. Either that or I'll often try directing my energy towards them- bringing a solid hand of critique and authority to try to discipline and correct them.

It turns out, according to the best research on adolescent development that teenagers don't respond well to negative critique. Bummer! It would be so much easier if it worked. But it doesn't. The more often and intense they feel negative vibes from someone, the more they will avoid them. Of course- it makes perfect sense. Why would anyone intentionally stay close to someone who criticizes them frequently and brings negative energy? Sadly, for many parent-teen relationships, that's the dynamic that gets set out of the gates and is really difficult to change.

So, what works? What works to both connect with our teens and also help them to grow, change, and adapt?

What works best is to flip the script and be on the hunt for the good, the true, and the beautiful in our kids. Here's what I mean:

- *Anytime our kid says something kind, we take note and make a big deal out of it*
- *Anytime our kid chooses to respond with patience rather than an eye roll or negative talk, we acknowledge it and show gratitude*
- *When our kid does something impressive, something that we would say is a degree of success that an adult should be able to, we notice and reflect on how impressed we are with them*
- *Anytime we catch them reading instead of being on their phones, taking a walk with a friend instead of playing video games, apologizing to a sibling for being rude, creating something artistic, or sharing a new fact they learned- acknowledge and celebrate it*

Recently, I was surfing with my son and on the way back to the parking lot, an older woman going by slowly on a bike turned to us and asked about the temperature of the water. Before I could respond, my son did, and with a really kind tone of voice, he engaged in pleasant small talk with her. He smiled, she smiled back, and she moved on. I, it turned out, didn't even say anything. He did it all.

Nobody grows through negative feedback or correction, despite what we think or have experienced. That only brings about compliance at best, mixed with some distrust and distance. People grow primarily through love and acceptance. And teenagers need a lot of it- just as much as they needed it when they were infants and toddlers but in a different flavor.

They live all day long in a world of rejection, comparison, and critique. At home, they need to balance that with exorbitant affection, connection, acceptance, and love. They will turn into whatever reflection you show them. So let's show them all the good, true, and beautiful parts.

What do you need to shift in order to give your kid or students more of what they really need?

The Critical Feedback Kids Need from Peers

"Bro- I can totally see you doing that someday!"

That came from one of the most beautiful and unexpected interactions I've ever witnessed, between two young guys in an Accounting class in the inner city. One kid was giving the other a spontaneous compliment, affirming an idea the other student had about his future. It was so surprising because just a few weeks prior, those kids had never spoken before, were suspicious of each other and steered clear of anything except for conflict. They were recruits in rival gangs.

Several years ago we were given a grant to work with students in an at-risk public high school and found an opportunity to work inside a school that was reportedly seeing their worst gang conflict in over a decade. We were invited to come weekly over the course of a semester to run our LifeScript course once a week with forty students. The teacher warned me,

"In my eleven years of teaching, I've never had worse students. They don't care about anything. Half of them won't even bring their textbooks to class. Kids come to class high. Some will walk out in the middle of class and not return. It's completely segregated; we've had death threats in the class from students in rival gangs. Good luck! You're going to need it."

I needed more than luck, perhaps a miracle. I walked in the first week pretty sure the program was going to be a complete failure because the only way the course would be effective was if we could create a new culture inside the large class- a culture of honesty, vulnerability, and open, respectful sharing with each other. The task was immense, but we leaned in.

Around the age of 12, the brain undergoes a massive reconstruction and kids experience gigantic shifts. For one, they start thinking abstractly and become self-conscious. They also change their focus of identity from their internal family to the external world; their peers. Their identity, worth, and sense of self is interpreted through the feedback they receive from- you guessed it, other kids who are also figuring out life for themselves.

It's a time in life of profound exploration of identity, beliefs, values, and roles and it's primarily driven by our experience of interacting with our peers. We experiment with everything all in search of discovering who we are, who really loves us, and how to best live in this world. We watch what other kids are wearing, listening to and laughing at and try to mimic the best we can for acceptance, approval, and internal resonance. We quit sports and activities we used to love and try new things. We retreat to our rooms, to our devices, and to social venues where we can be with our peers.

What an absurd idea, if you really think about it. We pull away from the very people who have wisdom in life, our parents and guardians, and look to our peers to help us make sense of everything. Our parents have fantastic insight into our talents, personality, obstacles and opportunities, and we'd rather hear what our friends say than what our parents think. But that's the way it works.

Which is why it's so critical to go with that flow. If adolescents need each other to make sense of themselves and this world, and will sacrifice their true selves in order to meet their needs for acceptance and belonging, what if we quit ignoring it and instead create a better structure?

There's so much posturing and pretending during the adolescent years- not in order to be deceptive but in order to preserve your sense of self and discover who you really are. On their own, teenagers don't have the experience or wisdom yet to know how to talk about those important dynamics, so they need a structure to engage well with each other. They need adults to demonstrate authentic self-disclosure and discovery. They need someone to guide them to the right questions and topics for discussion, to manage respectful sharing, model empathetic listening, and create the space for sharing.

Students will engage, we've learned that over the past twenty years. They want to. They will open up and share their stories, experiences, thoughts, fears, worries and dreams. They will learn from each other, borrowing from each other's language, values, ideas, and goals. When one kid shares openly, the other will, too. Vulnerability begets vulnerability. When one kid shares something private, something they've hidden for fear of rejection and doesn't receive rejection or confusion but instead is understood and accepted by their peers, they will flourish. And heal. And integrate the negative or painful experiences they've had into their life story, which is foundational to wellbeing and mental health.

Students need each other to grow up. But they need adults to guide them.

Rethinking Stress and Overwhelm

There's no question that students face a lot of pressure these days. Actually, students today are under a lot more pressure than their parents were at their age. The academic requirements to get into college have skyrocketed, and the increased pressure to be involved in clubs, service organizations, and sports, plus the demand for high test scores means that students are busier and more stressed than ever before.

In a recent survey of teen stress levels, about half of students are chronically stressed, with immediate and potentially long-term consequences on their emotional, physical, and mental health.

There's a real problem with stress today. Most adults don't handle stress well, and emerging adults are especially vulnerable to handling stress very poorly (think: lifetime habits formed, coping mechanisms like substance abuse, and subpar academic performance).

Students need support from their parents more than ever before.

In a development phase full of relationship transition, even though students are directionally pushing away from their parents in order to grow their sense of freedom, autonomy and form their own identity, they need their parents to stay close by, both physically and emotionally. They need their parents to do a lot more than help them manage their schedules and accomplish their tasks, they need their parents to check in on them, to stay close emotionally, and to be available.

A young college student told me recently: "I don't know if my parents really care about me. They definitely care about my grades, they care if I clean up after myself, and they care about how much money I spend and how much time I'm on my phone or my computer. But I'm not sure if they really care about how I'm doing."

The danger is that we create patterns in relationships where our only points of contact are over logistics and tasks and that our bond is superficial so they learn that their value is wrapped up in what they do, not who they are.

No matter what age or stage your kids are in, and no matter how much irritation they have for you, your kids need you to be safe for them and close to them.

Here's a brief overview of what safety looks like and feels like and how safe relationships grow between parents and their kids:

- *You share your struggles, hopes, and fears with them*
- *You contain their emotions when they share them*
- *You never overreact when they show big feelings*
- *You don't try to minimize or convince them they don't feel a certain way*

- *You demonstrate understanding and empathy and validate their feelings*
- *You mirror their emotions as they relate stories to you- your face looks surprised when they are surprised, your face looks sad when they tell you sad things, etc.*
- *You affirm that they are valuable, good, and loved with your words, actions, and affection*
- *You ask them questions about how they're doing, how they're feeling, what they're excited about and what they'rethey annoyed with*
- *You really listen to them, actively and with curiosity*
- *You pursue them continuously, even when they don't respond*
- *You give them appropriate space when they ask for it and let you know they need it- you don't smother them or shame them for wanting to keep things private from you*

Life is stressful, there's no doubt about that. And there's no doubt that transitioning into adulthood is extremely stressful, full of pressure and fear and confusion. Parents can offer the most significant support and encouragement and be life guides to their kids. Safe, close parents are a huge difference maker for kids who transition well into healthy, thriving adults.

Their Own Experience

When our oldest started Middle School, we quickly realized how little we knew about what he went through all day. Going to back-to-school night was helpful to get a glimpse into his world: who his teachers are, what the boys' locker room looks like, where he eats lunch, and what it's like to move between classes. We still see him a lot, but more and more we're discovering how little we actually understand what his life is like. Who are his friends? What does he do between passing periods? What jokes does he laugh at? What does he eat for lunch? What is he looking at on his friends' phones?

Like most parents who have teenagers, we've been learning that this is an extraordinary shift we're making, almost like we're having kids for the first time again. And just like when we first had a baby, not only were we unprepared for what was coming but the difficulty of the transition and so much of the stress has been about our own reactions to these changes.

It's really, really hard to have a teenager.

- *We feel like he's pulling away.*
- *We worry about the choices he's making.*
- *We're not sure who his friends are who are influencing him.*
- *We wonder if we should restrict his freedom, or give him more.*
- *We're worried if his natural kindness, patience, and sweetness will ever return.*

He's carving his own path now and it's different than the choices we made when we were his age- he has different interests, different values, different friends, different technology distractions, and different degrees of motivation.

But there are two things in a parent's control.

My Reactions. As parents, we can only control our own reactions, which includes paying more attention to feeling sad, rejected, angry, anxious or afraid about these drastic changes. For me, this looks like processing my feelings through journaling, venting productively with my wife, meditation and prayer.

My Perspective. We can also work to see our kids in a neutral light. We can reserve judgment about them and get to know who our kids are- on their own terms. We can stop superimposing our viewpoints, our values, our interests, our fears, our motivations onto them.

We can work harder to get to know them as they really are, independent, unique, and still developing. You might find your kids change their interests faster than some people change their socks- don't be shocked by their sudden change in focus, step back and wonder why. Make a lot of observations instead of accusations. Park your anxiety or fear to the side and instead explore what sparks they feel and what each of their ever-changing interests might say about who they're becoming.

The more you look at your kids with curiosity and neutrality, the more you will be able to see them as they are:

- Ask curious questions
- Make a lot of observations to yourself, to your spouse, and to your close friends
- Notice what they pay attention to

When you look at them you will start to see who they really are, which will then help you realize their unique attributes, qualities, personality, and path. Only then will you be better equipped to respond to their needs, to come alongside their interests, and to encourage them into their unique story.

Here's a helpful model you can use to better understand who your kids are and what they're going through:

Look > See > Realize > Respond

If you don't look at them neutrally to see who they really are, you'll likely get stuck in a pattern of having strong reactions to their choices. That means you'll probably create more distance in your relationship, and your kid will lose out on the value of your wisdom and affirmation. Look at their behaviors. See what's behind them. Realize what drives them. Respond to who they really are.

If you do work hard to look at each of your kids in order to see them and realize what they're going through, not only will you better understand who they are but you'll have many more opportunities to redefine closeness throughout the stages of their journey.

Modeling Healthy Friendships

Following a recent speaking event to a group of parents, a dad came up to me with a really concerned look on his face and asked me, *"What's the most important thing I can do to be a better dad to my two teenage boys?"* Out of my mouth came an idea that had been brewing for years and surprised me by how personal the implications were for my life.

Here's what I said, off the cuff: "You have at least one close friend, right? I bet your sons know that man, but I'm guessing they don't know him very well at all. Do they know him well enough to call him if they get into a jam? Does your friend actively, intentionally reach out to your boys to spend time with them, get to know them, and be open with them? I bet not. The most important thing you can do as a dad to your teenage boys is to deepen that friendship you have with that man, and be intentional about how you create experiences for your boys to be around the two of you, and clearly communicate to him as well as your sons that you want him to be more than a distant role model in their lives, but specifically invite him to become an active advisor, guide, and mentor."

As soon as I said it, I knew that idea was for me, too. Right when I got into my car in the parking lot, I called one of my closest friends and said, "Charlie, my son hardly knows you. He knows that we're friends, he sees you once a year at best, but at this rate there's no way when he enters his teenage years that he's going to call you to share something with you, ask you for advice, learn from you about how to live life, or even really know who you are. I want to change that. I want him to get to know you, to learn from you, and to learn about what good friendship looks like from how we interact. Would you be open to spending time with me and him a few times every year- we can go to a baseball game together, go bowling, fishing, camping- anything, really?"

Guess what Charlie said? *"100%, yes."*

Countless studies have proven the value of having close friendships with our psychological and physical health. People who have close friendships do better academically, at work, economically, physically, psychologically, and spiritually. Being connected to friends means you're less likely to feel depressed or anxious, more willing to take risks, and you'll make more money throughout your lifetime. On a research, logical level, I doubt anyone would challenge the benefits of close friendships.

Then why do so few people (adult men especially), have close, trusting friendships with at least a couple people? Why is loneliness on the rise so dramatically? We can point to the ubiquity of smartphones and social media as sources to our disconnection, but blaming them can only get you so far.

One of the foundational questions we guide people to process in The YouSchool is about their friendships and experience of belonging they have with others. We know the importance of meaningful friendships and have seen firsthand that even if someone can get clear about their purpose, career path, clarify their core beliefs, have a vision for a life of impact but they don't have close friends- then they still deeply long for more meaning in their lives. If we had to choose, we'd rather guide people to healthy, authentic friendships than to meaningful work.

In our work with thousands of adolescents through Middle and High Schools we invite them to reflect on their understanding of friendship, their experiences with friends so far in their lives, to project and imagine the kinds of friendships they'd like to have in their lives, and then define what kind of friend they commit to being to others. As a part of that process, we ask them to talk about how their parents have modeled friendship to them, and reflect on what they've learned from their parents as it relates to friendship. One thing we hear consistently, regardless of the demographics of the school, is kids talk about how they don't know if their dads have close friends at all. We hear that from inner city kids, students at continuation high schools, and students in high-achieving schools and wealthy neighborhoods.

As a simple observation, although friendship is an innate desire found inside everyone, the art of practicing healthy friendship is a skill that can only be learned by watching it modeled by others. If you don't learn from your parents how to have healthy friendships as adults, you're going to struggle to figure that out, too.

What did you learn about friendship from your parents?

Understand Their Family Narrative

"Well, that reminds me of my time in 'The War'..."

We had done it again. A family member sitting around the living room had said something that was slightly related to a current global situation, and my grandfather launched into his 1,000th retelling of one of his three 'war stories' from his time in the Army as a medic in World War II.

This time, though, even though I could retell the story in my sleep, I thought it would be important to listen carefully. I quietly pressed record on our video camera, and captured him retelling the story so we could remember forever, long after he was gone. His war stories have become a part of my story, legends that guide the kind of person I want to become.

One of the most important things families can give to the next generation is a clear understanding of their family narrative. Research has shown in recent years that the most predictive indicator of an emerging adult's emotional wellbeing and resiliency is an awareness of where they come from, and who they come from.

People need to understand that their lives have a deep foundation; that they come from somewhere and that their lives are continuing a story.

The stories don't have to be overwhelmingly positive either. In fact, there are different kinds of family narratives:

The ascending narrative: it's a story based on growth and accomplishments and overcoming the odds- "We came here with nothing, and look what we built."

The descending narrative: it's a family story based on what used to be, and what was lost. "We used to be something, we were significant, and then your grandfather lost it all."

The oscillating narrative: research shows that this is the most helpful, because it's the most true. It's a family story that tells the good and the bad, the accomplishments and the failures, the ups and the downs- "We've been through a lot, but we always stick together no matter what."

The oscillating narrative is not only the most honest, it's also the most valuable because the story actually helps you interpret current reality in a meaningful way. It enables you recognize that no matter what the current situation is, it's going to change. And regardless of the situation, you're going to make it through and be okay.

Some families are tempted to hide their stories. Secrets are kept to protect the innocent, and a false narrative is built. Don't do that- it's not helpful. People always find out the truth, and then it's even worse because significant trust is destroyed.

As your family gathers together, take some intentional time to recall and retell your stories. Here are some ideas for the stories that you can remember together:

- *Stories of relationships starting (ie. grandparents meeting, parents meeting)*
- *Birth stories and pregnancy stories*
- *Wedding stories*
- *Stories of when people died*
- *The origin of family traditions, games and nicknames*
- *Old pet stories*
- *First job, worst job, best job stories*
- *War stories*
- *Where-were-you-when stories: man landing on the moon, Challenger space shuttle, 9/11, etc*
- *School stories*
- *Getting in trouble stories*
- *First girlfriend/boyfriend stories*
- *Fist fight stories*
- *Drinking-too-much stories*

Nothing should be off limits, because nothing is wasted. Every story represents a reality, a lesson learned, and a new viewpoint on the world. Become the curator of stories this week; collect them and share them. The storytelling could become a new story in itself.

Reject Linearity

In the YouSchool world, Sir Ken Robinson is less of a knight and more of a saint. He's been saying provocative critiques about the frozen and ineffective state of education for a long time, and we've been swallowing the pill.

In one of his famously well-viewed TED talk, Bring on the Learning Revolution, Robinson says, "We have to go from what is essentially an industrial model of education, a manufacturing model, which is based on linearity and conformity and batching people. We have to move to a model that is based more on principles of agriculture. We have to recognize that human flourishing is not a mechanical process; it's an organic process. And you cannot predict the outcome of human development. All you can do, like a farmer, is create the conditions under which they will begin to flourish."

We're finding that many students are stuck on a path that's been carved out for them, and they grate under the pressures and expectations to conform. If they get good grades in math class, then they get a LOT of encouragement and unsolicited advice to pursue more math, regardless if they like it or not. If they've excelled in a sport, they're recruited to private lessons and travel teams and get on a track to college recruitment. Again, regardless if they feel joy while they play.

What happens, though, when kids are good at something they really don't enjoy? What if there are students who, like me, have learned how to get good grades in every class, making it pretty hard to pick a path that matches aptitude with passion?

Robinson reminds us that we're all overly enthralled with linearity, following the trajectory towards educational and career paths that "make sense", are "practical", and on paper make rational sense. But if you widen the lens to the broader concept of well-being, we might see things a bit differently.

Eliminate Unspoken Expectations

No one ever told me that I had to go be an Accountant, but I got the message. Nobody in my family ever sat me down and explained that people in OUR family were financial accountants, and that I was born to work in a specific trade and had no other option. But I got the message.

I got the message that accountants were respected folks. I heard loud and clear that they were respected, and financially well off, and they had enough money to afford taking care of their families and going on nice vacations and driving nice cars and living in gated communities and were really, really nice people.

I can't remember exactly when but one day I announced that I would go into finance, too. I would get a degree in business or accounting and go work for a public CPA firm. I think I was in middle school, maybe 12 or 13 years old. When I made the announcement I don't remember anyone saying anything in particular, I just noticed and felt a collective sigh of relief. "Ahh... okay, he's going to be alright. He won't be poor, he'll be able to take care of himself and his family, and we'll be really proud of him and his career."

So I walked down that path.

I remember asking for a subscription to the Wall Street Journal- when I was thirteen. I remember sitting my parents down to tell them that I was quitting soccer and baseball to focus on "country club sports" like tennis and golf, which would benefit my career. I remember reading management books- for fun- during summers. I remember getting summer jobs in major corporations' finance departments and ending up having six internships (all in finance or accounting). I only applied to one university, citing it was because "their Business school has a great reputation." When I declared my major in Accounting and minor in Finance, I remember sharing it proudly.

It was good for a while. It was good to have the respect of my parents. It felt good to hear them brag about me and listen to parents of my other friends say things like, "Wow- my son has NO clue what he wants to major in. What did you guys do so well?" I liked feeling like I was going somewhere. I felt proud of being on a path that had a secure and knowable future- a path that meant I could relate to my dad and wear the pride of my mom and that I could look a girl in the eye someday. I felt reassured knowing that I could guarantee to take care of our family for the rest of our lives.

No one ever told me I had to be an Accountant, but I got the message.

I got the message that it was what "good" people did. I got the message that people who were in other professions, like teaching, were never really well off financially and always struggled (and you definitely didn't want to struggle). I got the message that because I had good grades in those classes then it was double confirmation that I should go down that path.

But.

But, I always had this curiosity towards people. Ever since I was little, I was always fascinated with people's stories. I had an insatiable need to hear people talk about themselves. I was a listener, an observer, a reader, and a watcher. I loved hearing people talk about themselves, and open up about their thoughts and feelings and ideas. I loved it when people would tell me things, and then say things like, "I've never told anyone else that story before." I loved it when I could tell that someone felt cared for just because I was listening intently.

So when I was in my upper division classes in college, dead set on turning into an accountant and solidified in my path, things got quite confusing. I was doing well in my classes, getting some of the top grades. I was excelling in the on-campus recruiting process by outside public accounting firms, even getting offers for internships and jobs after graduation. But, when I was in my classes, all I was thinking about was the student organization I was a leader in. There, I had the opportunity in my spare time to lead, and speak, and mentor, and run teams, and plan events, facilitate retreats, to influence people's lives. Outside of class and my internships I got to feed my soul and listen to people's stories and inspire people and teach them.

I remember the day I called my parents to tell them that I wasn't going down the accounting path, and instead going to work for a non-profit doing leadership development with college students, required to raise funds for the organization and earn a fraction of what I was going to earn otherwise. On one hand it felt like I was letting them down, like I was a disappointment or a failure. But on the other hand, it felt like freedom. I was stepping out, onto my own path, to blaze my own trail and follow my passions. They never told me I couldn't, but I got the message anyway.

Cultivate Independence

Since the day they learn to walk and talk, kids yearn for more freedom. They simply want to do what they want to do when they want to do it. No wonder- *don't you?*

Do you remember the Burger King slogan from back in the day? It was a catchy little jingle: "Have it your way, right away, at Burger King- *now*." They captured the heart cry of all of us- especially those of us born and raised in the United States.

Other cultures seem to understand interdependence, service towards others, and humility better than ours. We are ingrained with a clear message: the good life is found on the other side of ultimate freedom.

Of course, true success, maturity, and wisdom look quite different. The most radiant people seem to be the ones who put others first, freely. They seem to have learned the secret to the game of life- it's not about you. Unfortunately, that's not a lesson learned early in life. In fact, it seems to be you have to grasp and be granted freedom before you can move to the phase where you start sacrificing your freedom for others.

Now, let's look at that dynamic when it comes to raising or working with teenagers. The problems and conflicts we have with them typically are a **clash of freedom and responsibility**. They want more space, but they prefer not to be held accountable. They want to do what they want to do when they want to do it, but they don't want to have to clean up after themselves.

It's a rough transition.

Good parents understand that it's our job to teach responsibility. We know they need to figure out life on their own so they can manage life on their own someday. So, we experiment by granting more freedom to them. Yes, it's an experiment, and yes, there are some explosions along the way. (How does the saying go? 'If you want to make an omelet, you've gotta crack a few eggs.')

We give them more freedom and try our best to communicate the expectations and the potential consequences, but inevitably there's a mismatch.

The central problem parents have is knowing when to grant freedom and when to keep both hands on the wheel. There's no manual for this, it's a case-by-case, almost moment-by-moment excursion. We don't know which choices will result in a life lesson, or a life ruined. We can't predict how consequences will cascade over time, and we easily project problems today with catastrophes a decade away.

Nevertheless, we let them have more freedom with their time- their bedtime, their free time, and their sleep schedule.

We let them have more freedom with their friendships and spending time with peers without supervision.

We let them make more choices with their devices.

But then, they blow it. Of course!

Like a pharmaceutical commercial, there are a few disclaimers: Teenagers are all gas and no break. They are prone to making impulsive decisions. They're thirsty for acceptance from their peers, and risky behaviors seem to correlate to more acceptance.

But it's through those experiences that they learn to manage freedom more responsibly. They learn that when they talk behind a friend's back- their friends drop them. They learn that when they choose not to study- they don't do well on tests. They learn that when they stay up late- they're incredibly tired the next day.

At least, we hope.

This raising humans thing isn't for the faint of heart. It takes tremendous resolve and relentless focus on the future state we're hoping for them: a life well-lived. We have to let them "feel, fail, and fall" (Shefali Tsabury, author of Conscious Parenting), and walk with them every step of the way.

What's the next area of freedom you need to give to your kids?

Realigning the Role of Adults

A 2015 survey of teachers in the United Kingdom asked over 1,000 teachers why they went into the profession initially, and 93% of them said they were motivated to make a difference in the life of a young person. The problem is, 93% of them also said they thought they'd be good at it, and 91% said they were attracted to teaching because they personally enjoyed the subject matter.

A generation ago and more, new teachers were attracted to the profession to invest in kids and make a difference in their lives. The job was a means to an end. Now, it's easy to get lost in finding personal fulfillment in the subject area just as it's easy to get lost with 150 students on your roster and more pressure than ever to get students to perform academically.

Teachers don't have as much freedom to engage with their students on a personal level as they used to. Or time. Most of them aren't taught how, or towards what end. Many work in a school where it's not celebrated, or encouraged, to personally connect with kids. When the bell rings, teachers move just as quickly to the parking lot as kids. Admin leaders are in their offices all day. The best ones always find a way. And there are always the best ones to find on every campus.

The primary role of a teacher is not to teach math, or language skills, or to get passing A.P. scores, it's to guide students to build meaningful lives. To the extent that a teacher sees that as their primary responsibility, definition of success and lens to work through, you will find students who are flourishing with caring adults supporting and challenging them along the way.

Life Guide Skills

Break the Plane

I remember Mr. Neeve, my 7th grade Social Studies teacher. He seemed so old at the time, but he was probably in his late twenties. What I remember about Mr. Neeve was his energy and passion for having us in his classroom- he greeted every student as they came through the door and seemed so excited to teach us something that day. Honestly, I don't remember if we had many personal interactions, but to this day I still root for the Cal Berkeley football team because he went to Cal and always talked about his love for his alma mater. Mr. Neeve was engaging, invited us into his life, told us interesting stories, and helped me discover a passion for history.

Breaking the plane in the classroom is a phrase we used to use a lot in education or in public speaking- the idea is that we walk through the invisible barriers that exist from the audience (students) and the sage on the stage (teacher). For many, there's comfort staying behind the desk, in the front of the class with a dry erase marker in hand. It feels more vulnerable and exposed to break the plane, walk up and down the rows, or to invite students into your life.

What happens to students when they feel personally connected with one of their teachers?

The best research shows that when students feel known and when they feel like they connect with their teacher, they do better academically. As one student put it, "I don't even like his subject, but because I feel like I know him I always try hard."

Here are a few questions for you to reflect on, ideally with a colleague after you've had the chance to write some of your own thoughts down:

- *What do you notice when there's a lack of connection with students in your class?*
- *Who are significant teachers from your life who modeled either active connection or disconnection?*
- *What do you find easy and natural or difficult and uncomfortable about breaking the plane?*

Nurture and Challenge

All kids have an inherent potential to achieve academically and flourish personally. They need to be challenged with high expectations to reach their potential. They will rise to the expectations you set for them, especially when matched with the right support, modeling, and encouragement. They also need to be nurtured and cared for, supported in their emotional development and identity formation.

There's so much pressure these days for academic achievement. Where perhaps a generation ago the rigor of intense academics was reserved for college prep private schools, now with the increased competition of college admissions and a collective call for all students to be college-ready, it's hard for a student to escape the rigor unless they really want to.

Perhaps it's become a little lopsided, though.

The number of students who feel personally connected to an adult on campus or known by an adult on campus has declined over the years. That's matched with increased student mental health challenges, anxiety, depression, and worse. Do they need a more challenging curriculum? Faster-paced schedules? More students taking more AP's so they can get ahead in college? Some do. And some don't. Regardless, every student, in order to grow and develop into their true potential will need both.

- *What's your natural style of working with kids- do you tend to be more nurturing or challenging?*
- *Who are the role models you had on either side?*
- *What worries or concerns would you have if you were 'too challenging' or 'too nurturing'?*

Active Listening: Seek Understanding

When you seek to understand what students are going through: what they care about, what their aspirations are, what their families are like, what challenges they face- it sparks a connection with them. Showing genuine interest and curiosity towards students and their personal lives will not only help you connect, but it will also help you create a better learning environment and learning outcomes.

The first time I ever had an adult who was interested in my personal life was during my second year in college. There was an older man on campus at USD who was the student organization rep for a club I was a part of, and I had signed up to serve in a leadership position the following year. Chris reached out to set up a meeting with me, sort of an interview to review the expectations for the role, and rather than a formal conversation I found Chris to be sincerely curious about me- what had led me to USD, about my family, about what I was interested in, and why I was majoring in accounting. I really enjoyed our conversation- I felt safe with him, understood by him, and when he offered to share some advice for me I was instantly open and engaged.

Most students don't feel understood- by anyone. A standard, natural part of the development process for adolescents prompts them to pull away from the primary adult relationships in their life to differentiate who they are and what their identity is on their own. It's healthy, but it causes some problems in their life. They inadvertently isolate themselves from the very people who hold wisdom about how to live well. Instead, they look to their peers, perhaps to social media 'influencers' and only potentially to other adults in their life.

That's where you come in. You might have a contract that explicitly states your job to teach learning outcomes in a single subject. However, your real job is to help kids grow up. You're responsible for creating an environment for them to discover and construct a meaningful life, which involves guiding them to reflect on their identity, their purpose in life, and on how to design supportive relationships with healthy people.

Active listening is more than just using nonverbal cues to encourage students to share more in classroom discussions. At its core, it's about leveraging your curiosity to guide them to reflect on the story of their lives- what they think about, care about, aspire to, worry about, and love.

- *What questions can you integrate into your lesson plans this week that demonstrate your curiosity for who they are, where they come from, and where they're headed?*

Active Listening: Validation

Can you think of a conversation you've had where you truly felt listened to on a deep level? Perhaps it was a conversation you had with a best friend, a new love interest, a therapist, or a bartender (you never know, right?). You don't forget those kinds of encounters- they stay with you for a long time.

- *Who's the best listener you know?*

There's something profound, almost spiritual, about spending time with someone who's skilled at listening. It's a scarce quality and skill, unfortunately. Active listening isn't just about nodding your head or repeating what you think you heard. It's about helping someone put words to their experiences and feelings, giving them a safe space to indeed be vulnerable, and creating a moment where their true selves can emerge.

- *Who do you feel safe with to share your genuine thoughts?*

When we create an experience inside the classroom for students to share their thoughts and feelings, we have an opportunity to do two things: (1) Without judgment communicate to students that their thoughts, ideas, feelings and perspective matters, is interesting, and has inherent value, and, (2) model to students what good listening looks like. Adolescents are going through a development phase where they're trying to discover who they are, what they believe, and what it looks like to live well. They need to experiment with different ideas, attitudes, and beliefs, and find out for themselves what resonates with them on a deep level. They need adults to validate their expressions and experiments, not adults who react (or overreact) with correction, judgment, anxiety, or shame. It might seem counterintuitive to some, but unless students can feel validated by the adults around them they won't be able to construct a well-formed identity.

There's a helpful ancient proverb that puts this principle into action: "Rejoice with those who rejoice, and mourn with those who mourn." The idea behind it is to celebrate with someone when something good happens in their lives and mourn with them when they experience a loss. It's easy to miss both opportunities, especially when you're around many kids throughout the day. But if you're looking for things to celebrate or things to grieve, you will start noticing more opportunities to connect with them and help students feel validated in what they're going through.

Who do you call when you have something to celebrate or something to grieve?

Listening well to students by validating them will help their brains connect the dots (fancy term: integration) and see more explicit patterns of meaning in their lives. You will help them feel understood, safe, and inherently valuable. You will help them process their emotions productively and find clarity in the experiences they're having.

Care Through Coaching
How do you help the kids who are working for the approval of others or the ones who are shut down? Again and again, you guide them to reflect on their lives, start writing about and talking aloud about their futures, creating space for them to imagine different scenarios and paths their lives might take. As they share their dreams and goals and aspirations, don't take them at face value- challenge them, ask students to explore more and explain why they care about that particular goal or direction, and fill out a deeper explanation.

Motivational Interviewing

It's a process derived from therapeutic work with folks in addiction recovery. Years ago, researches saw strands of data where some people were working through addictions more effectively than others, and pulling on those strands uncovered the underlying gem- when addicts were guided to reflect on who they wanted to be in the future, they found and maintained the motivation to go through the difficult work of recovery. That discovery has led to a process called Motivational Interviewing, which now has seen research-based merit in various domains, not just addiction recovery but also in education. MI is a relatively simple process anyone can employ to support and assist someone going through a challenge. You can learn it, too, and find that the kind of influence you have on students transcends content knowledge of your subject but extends into their personal growth, too.

We have an opportunity to support students as they grow through the most formative time of their lives, and the role we play is critical. What you will do to elicit the internal drivers of your students will help them find the why behind their actions, and it's worth the effort- for the sake of kids.

Modeling and Demonstrating

No matter how effective we are at breaking the plane, nurturing and challenging, active listening, telling dynamic stories, or helping them find their aspirations, we will NOT see students step fully into their potential for a meaningful life until and unless they see it modeled in us, first.

The most important thing you can do for your students is to live your life fully authentic, fully alive, and fully aligned to your purpose. Students need to see what it looks like to flourish, thrive, and live out a meaningful life in this world. They need to see what it looks like to have healthy relationships, stand up for beliefs and values, and invest talents and strengths for the greater good. They will not become who we hope they become until they have adults who model and demonstrate what it looks like in real life.

Yes, the pressure is on!

The pressure is on you. You've decided to say yes to the responsibility to help kids grow up into healthy adults- that's the primary job of teachers, coaches, and support staff in a school or organization that supports kids directly. Because you said yes to that responsibility, whether you were aware of it or not, it's an opportunity for you to find, define, and unleash a meaningful life on full display for kids to watch. And yes, they are watching.

Whatever you do, please continue to show up for your students, bringing as much passion and energy, nurture, and challenge as you can- for the sake of kids!

Using Stories to Build Connection
"I've been in his class since September, and he still doesn't know my name."
— Senior in high school (in late April, 2019)

Most students don't feel their teachers know them at the middle and high school levels. On one level, that's not a big surprise. A teacher might have 140+ students they see every week, so how could they get to know each student on a personal level? But let's take a minute to think about the student experience when they don't feel known:

- *When students don't feel known personally, they don't engage as much.*
- *When students don't feel known, they don't show up as often.*

- *When students don't feel known, they miss opportunities to learn.*

While a teacher might not have the time or capacity to get to know each student personally, they can do something to build more connection: **they can open up and share about their life.**

Ideally, a teacher would have the opportunity to sit down with every student for a personal, one-on-one conversation and get to know them, their life story, interests, learning style, personality, etc. When any adult pursues a kid individually with an attitude of curiosity and warmth (regardless of the reaction they get), there's good stuff that happens.

But even if you don't feel like you can take the time for personal conversations with every student, any teacher can open up in an authentic, genuine way about their personal lives and create a connection with the *entire* class all at once.

Typically, we hear some pushback to that idea. Teachers who say, "I'm not comfortable sharing my personal life with students." That's understandable (although finding a job where you don't have to interact with students would probably be a good career move!). It's undoubtedly vulnerable for students to get to know you, and not all of them will respond with kindness or understanding.

Rather, most of the discomfort we hear from teachers is not knowing what parts of their life would be most appropriate to share. Here are a few ideas:

- *Stories about your real-life struggles*
- *Stories about your life lesson moments*
- *Stories about your failures, fears, weaknesses*
- *Stories where you've pushed through setbacks to overcome challenges*

- *Stories that don't paint you with a heroic light*
- *Stories that are relatable and relevant to their life stage*

It's not that complicated, actually. It's something that every teacher can do every day- even math and science teachers (especially them, actually). Students want to know you, they want to connect with you, they want to feel understood and cared for by you, and if you open up your life regularly they will engage more, show up more often, and try harder.

You might just see their test scores and grades go up, too. But that's beside the point.

Reflection in Every Class

A few years back, I knew that it was time for a career change. It was time for a change in the trajectory of my life. I just didn't have the confidence that if I continued down the path I was on, I would find fulfillment, and I knew I needed a shift. But, in what direction, I had no clue. Sure, there were paths I had crossed off- I knew I wasn't going to be an engineer or a zoologist, but I was open to anything else. Go into healthcare? Sure. Pursue a career in human resources? Why not? Get an MBA and then into sales or management? Yeah- I could see that. The world felt expansive, and the opportunities all seemed like genuine possibilities. But I knew I didn't want to just experiment with my next step, and I didn't want to waste time down the wrong path. I wanted to be confident that it was a direction consistent with my true nature. The anxiety that I felt through that time in my life was intense. The curse of too many options, perhaps. I knew I needed to narrow it down, but how? I'd already taken every personality or talent assessment under the sun, all of them confirming what I already knew but none illuminating the right direction.

That's when I figured it out. I didn't need to focus my energy on exploring the options, and I didn't need to waste time having other people tell me who I am or what to do. I had all the answers within myself. There were very real and very important parts of me I hadn't integrated yet. There were moments from my past that could be used as signposts for insight into who I am at my core and show me the right path for my life. I needed to explore my past, search my memories for critical moments that stuck out, lay them all out, and find where the dots connected. I started journaling and daydreaming, recalling different memories and writing everything down, even if it didn't seem relevant at the time. At the end of that prolonged exercise, I took a step back to look at it all, and there it was, staring right at me: my path.

Nowadays, I get the privilege of working in schools with groups of teachers, parents, or students and guiding them to recall different memories from their past. Every time, no matter the context or whether they're adults or teenagers, I get the first reaction is like I'm an intruder. Most people are initially defensive, shut down, or closed off.

I've been thinking about using a more direct approach when I get started, something like, "We interrupt this regularly scheduled broadcast to invite you to break out of your autopilot mode, stop, and think about your life." Self-reflection disrupts their routine and the status quo, and I can always feel their resistance. I've learned to anticipate about half who are open, ready, willing, and able to be guided through such exercises in any group. They're the students who whisper to each other: "Would you rather be doing this, or another worksheet or boring slide presentation?" Then there's a quarter of the crowd who have no idea what I'm talking about and need to be convinced that self-reflection is relevant or valuable.

And then there's the rest- the ones who see no need and no value for self-reflection, at least at that moment. They're the trickiest, the ones with their heads down or frowns on their faces. A couple of weeks ago, a student raised his hand and said, "Is this some kind of trick or something? Why are you making us think about things?"

I'm convinced that we need to guide students to take frequent steps back to reflect on their lives. Remember, recall, and retell the moments of their lives that stick out to them as necessary, unique, odd, or meaningful. With a deadly cocktail of extreme academic pressure and insanely competitive college admissions in today's education climate, everyone sees the spike in mental health problems, social and emotional breakdowns, and not nearly enough balance. When students are tasked only to stay focused on the present moment and fixate on academic success, they will miss out on adolescence's richness, a necessary and beautiful season for reflection, maturation, experimentation, and discovery. If we don't dedicate significant, frequent time to guide students into reflection, we're going to keep heading down the path to a cultural implosion of our own making.

If we don't guide students to reflect, they will miss significant opportunities.

- *Without reflection, they can't see what path their lives are on*
- *Without reflection, they miss out on opportunities to connect the dots from their childhood*
- *They won't become self-aware about their life story, personal beliefs, natural talents, or interests*
- *They won't be able to organize their lives well to include what's most significant*
- *They won't be able to speak confidently about their convictions or make difficult choices when values collide*

- *They won't be able to celebrate meaningful moments*
- *They will carry into adulthood unresolved wounds*
- *They will march forward in someone else's direction about what makes for a happy life*

We have an opportunity to create space in every subject and learning environment for students to reflect on their past, present, and future. To remember and recall and retell the moments that have shaped them and, through structured conversation, learn how to make sense of who they are, how they're wired, what motivates them, and to see what story they find themselves in.

We can even do it in math class. Yep, and let's throw science in there, too. Math and science teachers can thoughtfully prompt meaningful self-reflection for students. They can take a few minutes to ask students to remember moments that have shaped their attitude and mindset towards math. Think back about the grades they've received, comments that have been made to them or about them in math, how they've felt as they worked out a more complex application of concepts. We can give them prompts like:

"When it comes to math, I..."

"When I am working through a complex math problem, I feel..."

"One time, in math class, someone said to me, you..."

"Compared to other subjects, in math I..."

From a personal, human standpoint, when a teacher takes the time to guide students through reflection exercises like these, they are creating space for them to be real and present. To acknowledge that at least half of what happens in math class happens underneath the surface is about self-confidence, mindset, identity, and how you see yourself and want to be seen. Teachers who carve out time for reflection like this will see grades improve academically. If you help students be more aware, present, vulnerable, and mindful about their inner lives and voices, they will be more attentive, take more risks, and engage more fully. You can flush out limiting beliefs, fixed mindsets, bruised egos, or unhelpful competition.

I remember a student admitted through an exercise above that he felt like "the dumb one" in the room. Math didn't come easily to him, his parents had recently arranged a private tutor for him, and he needed extra time to finish his tests. He felt ashamed and discouraged, and what do you think happened to his motivation to push harder? In this exercise, he opened up and shared that his peers and his parents validated what he was going through. They reminded him of how he had worked hard in the past and figured out the complex concepts. He felt the shame dissipate, heard from the other students that they all struggled in different ways, and didn't feel so alone. A few weeks later, his parents told me that his attitude had shifted entirely; he was self-motivated and doing better in the class.

The moments we've been through and the things we've seen and heard have shaped our understanding of ourselves. Putting those moments together and they become a story. Recalling those moments allows us to examine that story, perhaps to reinterpret it and even tell ourselves a different one, a better one.

If you're a teacher or an adult who works with students, you can build self-reflection moments into your lesson plans and guide students to make more sense of themselves. You can model it for them first and show them that vulnerable self-discovery is key to wellbeing and balance. You can carve out time for these moments and know that the time you spend is never wasted but stored up as growth and emotional health.

Redesign the College Admissions Process

College admissions have suffered an image problem over the past couple of years. There's plenty to be critical about since the Varsity Blues scandal and the upheaval that the pandemic put on college campuses.

But, ironically, there are still so many good opportunities for college admissions- primarily to shape how kids think about themselves.

Any college advisor worth their salt will tell you that college admissions officers are looking for well-rounded individuals for their schools. They don't just want high test scores; they want unique people with interesting stories. They want to see who you are, how engaged you are in your local community, and how you serve others.

Can you think of another time in life when you're asked to demonstrate your positive moral character?

In professional job interviews, we'll get asked about our work experience and how we understand teamwork, but we don't get grilled about how we serve our family or neighbors.

Most parents want their kids to go to four-year universities. Most students want to be accepted into good schools. There is an intense application process that can't be done last minute between here and there. You can't all of a sudden start acting like a good human while you're writing your application. It has to be an expression of who you are.

Most teenagers, though, aren't focused on their inner transformation. They're focused on finding acceptance from their peers, doing the work expected from them, and discovering new ways to express their freedom.

That's why it's such a critical opportunity for adults who work with kids- parents, teachers, counselors, and coaches. Since we know the college application will require them to tell an authentic story about their true selves, we can begin preparing them early to tell an accurate and compelling story. We can start asking them to respond to the common app essay questions way earlier than the fall of their senior year, prompts like this one: "Describe a topic, idea, or concept you find so engaging that it makes you lose all track of time. Why does it captivate you? What or who do you turn to when you want to learn more?"

The questions that we ask turn into expectations, signaling to them what's most important- that every kid becomes someone authoring a meaningful life.

It's not uncommon for older high school students to express cynicism towards applying for college. It's just so overwhelming, competitive, and mysterious.

It's overwhelming because there's so much to be done on your initiative. No one's going to do it for you. There aren't clear steps to take. There's tremendous cost and risk involved.

It's highly competitive- you know that there are only a few spots available, and your very close friends will likely be competing against you for those spots.

It's mysterious- everyone heard about the 4.6 GPA kid with high SAT scores who didn't get accepted to Boulder. Or U of A. Or wherever. It's not clear-cut who gets in and who doesn't.

Many of the students we've talked to feel discouraged and get cynical. Those aren't good ingredients or a helpful foundation to go through an incredibly stressful process.

In a recent Wall St. Journal opinion piece, <u>The Power of Purpose Driven Schools</u>, writer Mark Oppenheimer makes a case for why students need what he calls a 'self-transcendent purpose to help them stay focused and motivated. When we reach for goals for personal or selfish reasons (I want to be happy, I want to be successful), the theory is that we will run out of gas and motivation. Instead, if we find a broader, more meaningful purpose behind our pursuits, we'll last longer and be more resolute.

In other words, Oppenheimer says, 'for those with self-transcendent goals, not for those with self-centered goals: "I want an education to help others," not "I want an education to get a good-paying job."' There's a body of research that asserts kids will learn more, stay focused longer, and push through setbacks if they believe the work they're doing matters on a larger scale than just their own life.

That's a problem for college admissions and students preparing to go through the application process. The message they're told is, "This is your future, your life- you need to find what makes you happy and pick a school that you love." Apparently, for most students, that's not enough. Many are opting out of the rigorous process, choosing an easier path, a path of less resistance, overwhelm, or anxiety.

I chose a school I knew I would get into, hands down. I had no concept of going to school to earn an education that would give me the capacity to make a difference down the road, and I was so overwhelmed by the thought of trying to get in somewhere selective and getting rejected and everyone finding out about it that I chose something easy.

So, what if we re-framed the transition from high school to college? Deep down, every teenager longs to know that they matter, their life counts, and they have inherent value to the world. They also are keenly aware of their youth, their lack of experience, and their inability to express a real contribution- yet.

What if the college admissions process wasn't just a game to try to win- what if it was a necessary step to finding a path towards making the world a better place?

What if we told students, "The world needs you to work really hard right now, put your head down and apply as well as you can to great schools. This isn't about you and your happiness, this is about the contribution we need you to make."?

CONCLUSION

After working with thousands of students for the past few years we have realized that many well-meaning, supportive parents aren't helping their kids as much as they think they are. About half of the students we work with have clearly received a specific message from their parents that only a defined career path will be acceptable and respected. Half of students have been told they ought to become doctors or lawyers, attorneys or teachers. Since their parents give them specific direction, they feel like they now are under a lot of pressure to live up to their expectations, and fear that they don't have the capacity and ability to please their parents.

But what about the other half?

They have been given no direction at all- and it's even harder for them. Their parents tell them a very simple refrain: "We don't care what you do- we just want you to be happy." It sounds great, doesn't it?

But, telling your kids you want them to be happy actually does more harm than good.

I get it, though. With three kids, when I imagine their future I don't feel invested in the kinds of career paths they walk down. I want them to figure out what their talents and interests are, and find a creative way to make money doing something they enjoy. I do NOT want them to feel pressured to please me, or teach them a false social hierarchy that only respects prestigious careers and pursuing wealth and keeping up with the Joneses.

Here's why parents tell our kids we just want them to be happy:

- *We mean it*
- *We don't want to put pressure on our kids to live up to false expectations*
- *We suffered under the expectations our parents put on us, and we want our kids to have a different experience*
- *We aren't sure what else to say*
- *It seems like something we're supposed to say*
- *We want them to feel what we do*
- *We want them to experience and feel what we've never felt*
- *We aren't sure how to help them find their way*

When we work with students who tell us their parents tell them they want them to be happy, they also admit to us that it's a really frustrating and unhelpful thing to say. Let me repeat that: they don't like it, nor is it helpful, to tell them you want them to be happy. Why?

Most parents haven't helped their kids know what happiness means or looks like- if they don't see you be happy, they won't know how to find it

Kids need honest, unbiased feedback from people who know them well to help them understand who they are, what their talents are, and what they're capable of

Kids know they need to find a job someday, they know they need to support themselves financially. That's already a lot of pressure. They don't need even more pressure also to find happiness.

To summarize everything, here's how we can help kids:

- Define happiness yourself by discovering what it means and demonstrating it to your kids consistently
- Think reflectively about your kids and what you notice about them. Take notes about what you see in them. Make observations about their talents, when you notice them come alive, and when you observe them suffer through tasks that drain the energy out of them
- Set them up with an unbiased but trained guide who can lead them through a process to discover for themselves who they are, what's most important to them, what kind of life they imagine for the future, and develop a plan to get there

We all want kids to be happy. We all want them to get off the family payroll someday, too. Do what's most helpful for your kids- live your life to the fullest, point out in them what you see, and learn to come alongside them in new and different ways.

The Punchline

It took all of these pages to finally get to this book's summary. I run the YouSchool- a company dedicated to helping You figure Yourself out. The name is a misnomer, though, and always has been. Here's the punchline:

It's not about you.

Maybe read that a few times slowly. The point of life is to put others before yourself. It's to set your sights on solving a problem that will contribute to the greater good. It's about investing your time, talents, energy, and resources into the service of something bigger than yourself.

Everything else falls into place once we recognize that and decide to pursue a life committed to the service of others. That vision, combined with the lives we lead as examples, will be the mortar that holds all the bricks together for kids to build a strong foundation.

ACKNOWLEDGMENTS

This book is a labor of love over many, many years. Even at a young age, I knew I was a writer. But, for too long, I listened to that voice that so many of us struggle with- the impostor. Every time I wrote something and went to post or publish it, I heard whispers: "Who do you think you are? Do you actually think people want to hear what you have to say?" Despite my outer confidence (some say cockiness), I internally wrestled with my ego.

Thankfully, I've had encouragement along the way to step into my authentic story and pursue my personal mission. It's the gospel I've been preaching, so I might as well listen.

But no affirmation has meant more to me than the people who know me the best- my family. To my wife, Caroline, thank you for always seeing the best version of me and being my lobster. To my mom, my editor and first cheerleader, thank you for reading every word I've written and helping me write better. Thank you to my kids, Cale, Grace, and Jane, for being my muses- learning about myself as I've tried to parent you has shaped me more than anything else in the world. To my sister, thank you for being such a great role model, friend, and comrade in life. To my dad, your example of hard work and dedication has paid dividends for both me and generations to come.

I've had the best guides in my life, too. To Sheryl Fleisher- who would I be without you? To Chris Nichols, you were the first person outside my family to see something greater in me than I saw in myself. I shudder to think who I would've turned out to be if it hadn't been for you.

The work of the YouSchool wouldn't exist without my two brothers from other mothers, Shawn Parr and Gregg Imamoto. Many years ago, you met a cynical punk kid, and for some reason, you believed in me and never wavered in your support. I only hope I've made you proud of what we've built together. There's also an extended cast of characters who've come alongside the YouSchool journey over the past decade whose names are written on the planks- your contribution matters.

Lastly, I need to mention the friends who, like brothers, make my life rich and joyful. To Caleb, John, Darrell, David, Charlie, Nic, Mike, Brad, Michael, Caden, Tyler, and Joe (in no particular order!)- knowing that you couldn't care less about what I do for work reminds me who I truly belong to.

There are many other people to acknowledge, too. People who mean a lot to me and have shaped my perspective and the content of this book: family members, friends, colleagues, and people I've never met- authors, researchers, and leaders I look up to, thank you.

ABOUT THE AUTHOR / ABOUT THE YOUSCHOOL

Scott Schimmel is the President and Chief Guide of The YouSchool, an organization committed to demystifying what it means to build a meaningful life. He also serves as faculty for transitioning veterans from the special forces. Scott's a frequent speaker, writer, curriculum designer, and consultant and has spent 20 years studying human flourishing in young adults. You can connect with Scott professionally on LinkedIn, sign up for the YouSchool's weekly email newsletter on their website, or see infrequent photos of his growing family on Instagram.

The Critical Foundations Curriculum: as you've read previously, each of the thirty critical foundational questions has a level of depth and nuance. You can try to answer each question directly. Still, in my experience, you need to be guided more deliberately through a series of other questions to clearly and confidently answer the critical one. That's why we put together the Critical Foundations Curriculum- available through weekly videos- short talks and interviews, accompanied by guided reflection and discussion worksheets. You can use it on your own, with your kid, or with a group of students. Get access to the curriculum at theyouschool.com/store

The Meaningful Life Checklist: if you'd like to download a visual guide to the thirty questions we've covered, go to **theyouschool.com/checklist** to download your copy for free.

Made in the USA
Las Vegas, NV
16 August 2022